AIMLESS

A 30-DAY JOURNEY WITH JESUS TO TRIUMPH OVER BLAH AND FULFILL YOUR PURPOSE

BRIAN S. HOLMES

Brian S. Holmes is the president and lead pastor of MPowered Christian Ministries, an evangelical ministry dedicated to promoting global revival by mobilizing disciples to advance the Kingdom of God globally. They provide a variety of speaking and counseling services, educational training, and free resources.

https://MPoweredChristian.org

AIMLESS first published by MPowered Christian Publishing 2023
Copyright © 2023 by Brian S. Holmes
ISBN: 978-1-7352423-6-1

All rights reserved. No part of this publication may be reproduced, stored or transmitted in any form or by any means, electronic, mechanical, photocopying, recording, scanning, or otherwise without written permission from the publisher. It is illegal to copy this book, post it to a website, or distribute it by any other means without permission.

Brian S. Holmes asserts the moral right to be identified as the author of this work.

Brian S. Holmes has no responsibility for the persistence or accuracy of URLs for external or third-party Internet Websites referred to in this publication and does not guarantee that any content on such Websites is, or will remain, accurate or appropriate.

Designations used by companies to distinguish their products are often claimed as trademarks. All brand names and product names used in this book and on its cover are trade names, service marks, trademarks and registered trademarks of their respective owners. The publishers and the book are not associated with any product or vendor mentioned in this book. None of the companies referenced within the book have endorsed the book.

First Edition published in Clearwater, Florida by MPowered Christian Publishing in August 2023. This book is manufactured in the United States of America. For permission requests, or information about discounts available for bulk purchases, sales, promotions and educational needs, contact publisher at: 2655 Ulmerton Road #178-5, Clearwater, FL 33762, or visit https://MPoweredChristian.org/publishing

Edited by Brian S. Holmes
Cover and book layout design by Brian S. Holmes
Nonprofit Design and Marketing > Effective Advertising Solutions, visit https://EASinteractive.com

Unless otherwise indicated, all Scripture quotations are taken from:
(NIV) Scripture quotations taken from Holy Bible, New International Version®, NIV® Copyright 1973, 1978, 1984, 2011 by Biblica, Inc.® Used by permission. All rights reserved worldwide.

Where (ESV) is noted the Scripture quotations are from:
The ESV© Bible (The Holy Bible, English Standard Version®), copyright © 2001 by Crossway, a publishing ministry of Good News Publishers. Used by permission. All rights reserved.

DISCLAIMER: This book is intended for informational purposes only, with the understanding that no one should rely upon this information as the basis for medical decisions. Anyone requiring medical or other health care should consult a medical or health care professional. Any actions based on the information provided are entirely the responsibility of the user and of any medical or other health care professionals who are involved in such actions. Although every effort to ensure that the information in this book was correct at press time and while this publication is designed to provide accurate information in regard to the subject matter covered, the publisher and the author assume no responsibility for errors, inaccuracies, omissions, or any other inconsistencies herein and hereby disclaim any liability to any party for any loss, damage, or disruption caused by errors or omissions, including but not limited to special, incidental, consequential, or other damages, whether such errors or omissions result from negligence, accident, or any other cause. This publication is not meant as a substitute for direct expert assistance. If such level of assistance is required, the services of a competent professional should be sought.

CONTENTS

GETTING STARTED

Introduction to 4D Devotional Series   1
Introduction to AIMLESS   5
Tips for Better Results   6

YOUR 30-DAY JOURNEY

Day 1 - Where Is Your Life Going?   11
Day 2 - The Empowered Christian Road Map (Your Life Blueprint)   16
Day 3 - What's the Purpose of Life?   22
Day 4 - You've Been Given An Incredible Opportunity!   27
Day 5 - A Final Destination Worth Striving Toward   32
Day 6 - Why you Must be Born Again to be Saved   37
Day 7 - Understanding the Process of Salvation   42
Day 8 - What does it Mean to Be a New Creation in Christ?   48
Day 9 - How Satan is the Saboteur of Your Journey   54
Day 10 - The 4 Main Ways Satan leads people to Hell   60
Day 11 - Close these 8 Open Doors and Keep Satan Out   66
Day 12 - 8 Keys to a Mindset for Emotional Health and Success   73
Day 13 - The 4 Habits of the Emotionally Resilient Christian   79
Day 14 - 8 Lifestyle Behaviors of the Emotionally Resilient Christian   85
Day 15 - The Fruitfulness of your Life Shows Your Direction   92

Day 16 - God Demands Moral Righteousness and Justice	97
Day 17 - Are Good Works Evidence of your Saving Faith?	102
Day 18 - The Christian Mission is Not to Fix the World	108
Day 19 - Your Mission as a Disciple of Jesus	113
Day 20 - 4 Keys to Run your Spiritual Race well	119
Day 21 - Who and What is The Church?	125
Day 22 - What are the Basic Functions of the Local Church?	130
Day 23 - How to go from Healthy to Empowered Church	135
Day 24 - What's your Identity and Calling?	141
Day 25 - How to Be Empowered for your Mission	147
Day 26 - How to Improve Your Life using TECRM	152
Day 27 - How to Make Disciples using TECRM	157
Day 28 - How to Make Better Decisions using TECRM	162
Day 29 - How to Prioritize Your Life using TECRM	167
Day 30 - God's Answer to Your "Why?" (Fan or Disciple?)	172
Notes	178
Afterword	179
Road Map Resources	180

Introduction to 4D Devotionals

4D Devotionals Series is a collection of 30-day Christian devotionals, each with a unique theme. 4D stands for an emphasis on being **D**aily, having **D**epth, with the goal of **D**iscipleship, and a **D**rive towards personal or mission action.

DAILY

God didn't create us to be mindless robots who just follow the rules. We were created to be free, sentient spiritual beings who would have relationship with Him forever. He desires us to know, love, and relate to Him with all our heart, mind, soul, and strength (Mark 12:30). He desires us to know Him through His Word, His Church, and His Spirit, and and have a lifestyle of worshipping Him in spirit and truth (John 4:24).

Right beliefs and lifestyle are important but they're simply the means to a higher goal: a right relationship with God. Like all good relationships, if you want to build it you need to desire it, be intentional, and make time to work on it with Him. You need to allow Him to get to know you, let down your emotional walls, not hide behind lofty and vague religion. You need to be real and share your authentic self with Him.

For every one born again, God lives in them and is always with them. You might ask, if God's with us the whole day is it still important to have *dedicated* time for devotion, Bible reading, prayer, etc? Yes, just because we have quantity time with God doesn't mean we have quality time with Him.

Private quality time with God is one of the best ways to develop your relationship and have greater intimacy (closeness). Consider the difference between just spending time with a loved one doing an activity together vs. spending quality time with them face-to-face, entrusting them with your deepest desires and most intimate secrets. There's greater spiritual revelation and supernatural life transformation in God's presence. Pursue encounters with Him daily.

DEPTH

I've had new believers learn from our ministry a few months and be shocked to discover that they know things and have experienced changes that people who've been Christians for decades haven't. This is because many sermons and popular books are often surface-level and trying not to offend people.

However, unshakable faith and dramatic transformation require us to unpack the deep philosophical truths of God, Bible, theology, doctrine, apologetics against false beliefs, and application of these truths. The goal of this series is to provide the content and activities to make this possible while still keeping it concise enough to be understandable and convenient.

Most devotionals are 1-2 minute personal stories offering a thought to ponder. Sure, something is better than nothing, but we shouldn't give in to this type of bare-minimum thinking. Settling in this way is one of the reasons why many Christians are not living spiritually free, and why there's a lack of spiritual growth and fervor in many churches. It's a red flag if you're only willing to give God two minutes of your day. This indicates that you're not truly pursuing God, lack rightly placed priorities, or have an unbalanced, unsustainable schedule packed with too many things.

Some people go to the other extreme - spending several hours a day with God. Most people just don't have the time, discipline, or patience to do this. Yes, God may lead you to do this on occasion, or during a pressing season, but this should be the exception, not the rule. Don't be a spiritual monk, isolated and disconnected from the world. Be a part of a spiritual community that is on mission together in the world.

There's a healthy balance between these extremes. Spend time daily in isolation and with God to recharge—then get back in the game! I recommend between 20 minutes and 1 hour as a good range for your regularly dedicated daily time with God. Our daily devotional readings and assignments take 20 minutes. Begin there, then add in additional Bible reading, worship, prayer, journaling, communion, etc. according to your preferences or as God leads.

Daily reading average 10-12 minutes. Some are sermon-like, offering wisdom, encouragement, and practical tips. Others are more like a theology class in Bible school. Still, some are practical ministry training to equip you to live more like a disciple of Jesus. While each 30-day book has a single theme, each day is independent and teaches a single topic. Topics are introduced and then broken into sub-points for easy comprehension.

The Bible is quoted extensively and verses are often referenced, easily providing some direction if you would like to include additional Bible reading that day. Prayer and journaling assignments are also included each day to help you discuss the topics with God and apply them to your life.

DISCIPLESHIP

A lot of popular devotional content is surface-level Christianity or merely pseudo-Christian, moreso about just improving your life or becoming a better person. This will not secure or sustain you. We must progress from being newborns needing the spiritual milk of elementary Bible truths, wise advice, positive thinking, and motivational encouragement, into mature adulthood consuming solid spiritual food (1 Cor. 3:2). We must progress from being self-centered people wanting God to give us what we want into disciples of Jesus asking God what it is that He wants.

Jesus said to make disciples and teach them to obey what He taught (Matt. 28:19-20). God wants us to be transformed from the inside-out (Matt. 5). We've been predestined to be conformed to the image of Jesus (Rom. 8:29). God's objective is to make us like Jesus in every way. It's not even about believing the right things, or behaving the right way, but becoming like Jesus through supernatural personal transformation. While each lesson will focus on something what they all ultimately have in common is that there is a way to approach the subject in a way that will make you more like Jesus.

The goal of all lessons is to push past the superficial level to get to root issues hindering your spiritual development. To destroy the ways Satan and your sinful desires are keeping you in bondage to your old nature. All lessons will either lay or build upon the foundation and core truths that shape your worldview and how you live. Not only learning but acting upon what leads to repentance, sanctification, spiritual growth, and personal growth.

DRIVE

It's the vision of my ministry to mobilize disciples of Jesus to advance the Kingdom of God globally. No educational program would be complete without action steps for practical application. As one person said, to know and not do is really not to know.

In ancient times, most children out of grade school learned to either follow the trade of their parents or they left home to apprentice under someone else and do on-the-job training. But in the modern era of education, much of the time students are in school they're spending thousands of hours learning and memorizing facts to take tests in subjects they have zero interest in pursuing a career in. What a horrible waste of intellect, time, energy, and money.

This false, harmful mindset has carried into the church as well so believers are just spectators who continue to learn but never do. Christians have not been given the option of being a learner alone. We're to be disciples that make disciples! We're not to be hearers alone, but doers (Jam. 1:20). Even the highly anointed, gifted, and compensated leaders are not to do all the work themselves. They are to equip the rest of the saints to do the works of the ministry (Eph. 4:11-12). That's you!

Every lesson is actionable. Some lessons will be more knowledge-based and others more action-based. But at the end of the day, I'm not teaching—I'm training! The goal is to help you discover, be prepared, trained, and mobilized to do whatever the Lord has called you to.

Introduction to AIMLESS

A 30-DAY JOURNEY WITH JESUS TO TRIUMPH OVER BLAH AND FULFILL YOUR PURPOSE

Do you feel confused, lost, and stuck? In as little as 20 minutes a day for 30 days, you can triumph over your lack of direction and start discovering and fulfilling your life's purpose.

AIMLESS captures the best from my 200,000-word landmark work, *The Empowered Christian Road Map: A Guide for Evangelicals: 8 Key Principles for Unswerving Faith, Laser-Focused Direction, and a Life Driven by Purpose and Action.* The most important and impactful things have been organized and optimized to be more understandable and implementable right away.

In a single, short, daily activity, AIMLESS delivers unchanging biblical principles, deep pastoral and philosophical insights, and practical action steps to prioritize and transform your life.

Life-changing yet shockingly convenient, this step-by-step blueprint will unlock your understanding of the Christian life, invigorate your day, and ignite your purpose as a disciple of Jesus.

REFUSE TO BE AIMLESS!!!

Tips For Better Results

You could just read this like a book but there really is so much more available if you truly do treat it like a 30-day daily journey with Jesus. I hope you do want to get the most out of this journey!

YOUR HEART POSTURE MATTERS

If you're just trying to check the "religion box" on your to-do list, and you and God both know it, you're not going to get much out of that time.

If the reason you're doing this is to prove to God, others, or yourself that you're a good person, that is a bad reason. If you're trying to help earn your salvation, or make up for sins you've committed by doing this, it won't accomplish that. If you're going to refer to this activity later as a reason why God owes you something that you want in return for what you did for Him, you're wrong for doing that. He doesn't owe you anything. You won't get credit from Him or be spiritually blessed if you're doing it for all the wrong reasons. Either come correct or don't come at all.

That being said, when you realize that you have sinful, selfish desires you can bring these to God, too. Before you even begin the reading portion, just start by acknowledging and confessing these things in your heart and ask Him to remove them. He would rather have a broken person honestly admitting their sins and faults, desiring to be holy, and knowing that they need Jesus, than a self-righteous person who arrogantly thinks they're already good.

It's also OK if you're still tired and need to wake up, or if you still have distractions or pressing concerns still on your mind you're having a hard time shaking. That's not a wrong-heart issue, it's a being-human issue. God's pleased by your willingness to meet Him for your scheduled appointment even when it isn't convenient. This is also what a fast does. It's an intentional denial of comfort to focus on God and draw spiritual sustenance from Him. You can take advantage of this discomfort when it happens organically.

Perhaps you may find yourself having mixed motives and emotions, that's OK too. You're likely going to learn new things and be challenged. Don't run away, bring those things to God and talk with Him about them. Perhaps you're new to this "meeting God" type of thing, that's OK too. Just have enough faith to keep trying and believe that God could encounter you this way. As a man once told Jesus, *"I do believe; help me overcome my unbelief!"* (Mark 9:24)

Just be honest with God about what you think and how you feel. Remember the goal is real relationship. Some of the conversations that help us get the closest with others were those that were the most difficult. So don't avoid God when you have mixed feelings, anger, bitterness, sadness, confusion, etc. Do the as the psalmists do in the book of Psalms, and talk to God about how you really feel. He wants you to be real and honest.

Just bring an earnest and sincere desire to glorify Him, spend time with Him, and become more like Jesus. Do this, and He will meet with you and you will be blessed and enriched by your time together.

SET THE ATMOSPHERE TO MEET WITH GOD

Get rid of distractions. This is especially important if you're only planning for 20 minute devotion time. Do your best to give God your undivided attention. If the phone itself is an easy distraction for you, or will interrupt with notifications leave it in the other room. If you're using a phone or tablet to read this book put it on airplane mode or disable notifications in some other way so that they don't interrupt.

If your spouse, children, roommates, pets, etc. will be a distraction, plan your devotional time at a time and place away from them. Remember to use the restroom or let the dog out before you get started. Get out your Bible, journal, pen, coffee, communion elements, or anything else you need so you have it available and won't have to stop what you're doing to get it later.

You could use candlelight instead of regular light. If you don't have scented candles you could also use incense or fragrant anointing oil to fill the area with a fragrant aroma. If you can find a cinnamon variety it's even closer to the fragrance formula God gave to Moses to use for special sacred purposes. These things are optional but do help set the ambience.

You could also put on instrumental worship music. Occasionally I'll feel led to choose a certain song and worship and sing to the Lord, but more often I pick playlists without any lyrics to use as background music. This helps me when I'm reading and focus my thoughts on hearing from God more clearly when I'm journaling.

SATURATE EVERY DEVOTIONAL TIME WITH PRAYER

The goal is not to simply do a reading assignment but rather to meet with God. If you just jump in it's very easy to turn these lessons into a homework activity. Begin every meeting time with a short prayer. It doesn't matter if it's only 10 seconds. In your own words, invite God to meet with you, lead you by His Spirit through everything, and to guide your focus and thoughts. I've included a closing prayer at the end of every reading portion. Feel free to add more prayer at the end as you feel God lead.

Also be "prayerful" (prayer-full) during all the rest of the reading as well. Prayer is just communication with God. It's us talking with Him and Him talking with us. So be open and receptive, even while reading, for God may interrupt your thoughts throughout the process. If He does, trust Him and go with it. Journal about what He's saying as well as your responses, thoughts, and feelings. It's ok if God takes you somewhere else. You can always return to continue reading where you left off after.

BE EXPECTANT THAT GOD WILL SHOW UP

God lives in you and is with you. If you have a sincere desire to meet

Him, and are doing it for the right reasons, He's faithful, He will show up.

He may speak audibly but more often than not He speaks by guiding our thoughts and impressions. Have your journal out and write down the impressions that come to you. Write down your prayers to Him. Write down how you feel and what is standing out to you about the lessons.

Each daily devotional has journaling questions related to the lesson. Start there but feel free to add additional things as you feel led. Write the date and time in each journal entry so you have a record of it. It will also help you notice patterns later of what works best for your time with God.

I CHALLENGE YOU NOT TO SKIP AHEAD

Don't read Day 1 yet! Wait until tomorrow. If you don't already have a daily routine try to establish one that you will stick with. This is important because I want you to also build spiritual discipline by having a daily routine. And when you finish the daily lesson if you want to keep going, supplement it with additional journaling, Bible reading, worship, prayer, intercessory prayer, etc. Don't jump ahead and do the next days lesson! Use patience and self control, two fruits of the Spirit (Galatians 5:22-23).

All too often I see ambitious A-type personalities cram a ton of reading, videos, classwork, etc. only to not fully retain it later. I've had to reteach things people already learned but it didn't stick because they did too much all at one time. There's a reason all long term success is gradual. If you want to lose 100 lbs develop the habits that will lead to losing 2 lbs a week for the next 50 weeks. The fad diets don't work long term, most of the weight coming back again. Likewise with many weight loss surgeries. This is because they never dealt with the root beliefs and behaviors that led to the problem in the first place. You didn't get your problem overnight and you're not going to solve it overnight. It's the same way with spiritual growth. Get good at the fundamentals.

Jesus spoke to an agrarian culture so He used farming metaphors a lot. Can you picture a farmer trying to cram? Make up for a bad last season by trying to rush and make the harvest come sooner. No, it doesn't work that way. He needed to sow seed and then nurture it for months until the harvest time was ready. Our spiritual growth is the same way. You can't cram and rush the process. So don't binge out and finish this book in a weekend. Don't start until tomorrow and then take the full 30 days.

You will be blessed by the process!

P.S. Still want something to do today? Plan out tomorrow. Set yourself up for success. Plan what time you will do your devotional and what you want to have with you (journal, pens, etc.). Get everything ready today so you don't have to worry about it tomorrow. Planning on waking up early? Go set your alarm now (and maybe your backup alarm). Set your coffee timer. Planning on doing it at lunch time or after work? Plan your contingency plan. What will happen if you get stuck working through lunch, need to pick up the kids or run errands after work, or some other unforeseen thing requires you to change your plans? Plan now what your backup plan for your time with God is going to be. This is one way to get control over your life even when you can't control everything.

Day 1

Where is your life going?

You ever wake up in the morning and think to yourself, "what am I doing with my life?" Perhaps you're so lost and confused just knowing you're at least going in the right direction would be a huge help. This lesson you'll learn what the Bible teaches about your current trajectory, the different options at the end of the road, and what you should do about it.

WHAT IS YOUR CURRENT TRAJECTORY?

Perhaps the gurus tell you to forsake all attachment and desire and pursue oneness with the universe to be released from the cycles of reincarnation. Perhaps you're following the way of Muhammad and hoping to be good enough on Judgment Day to go to Paradise. Hopefully you've already found Christianity, that would be good - because it's the one true path!

What you believe about Jesus and what He wants from you matters a lot. Perhaps you were told God loves you just as you are and has a wonderful plan for your life? Perhaps you've heard a preacher say God just wants you to be happy, healthy, and wealthy? If you're still living in sin, or like you exist to chase worldly pleasures, then you're still on a dangerous trajectory.

Did you know most people believe they're already a good person and they're probably going to go to Heaven? Do you know what the Bible actually says? It says we're all depraved sinners, and that if we don't turn from our former sinful ways; putting our trust in Jesus's divinity, death, burial, and resurrection; and live a Spirit-led life of obedience and righteousness with Him as Lord, we won't.

It describes the fallen state of all humans before they're born again like this in Ephesians 2:1-3:

> *"You were dead in your trespasses and sins, in which you used to walk when you conformed to the ways of this world... All of us also lived among them at one time, fulfilling the cravings of our flesh and indulging its desires and thoughts. Like the rest, we were by nature children of wrath."*

By children of wrath it means that we're literally born in a cursed state so that the way of evil seems good, right, and tempting to us. God's law doesn't make us good—it's necessary just to help restrain our naturally evil desires. We are therefore under God's judgment and wrath.

Jesus acknowledges the inherent evil desires of humanity all while telling us to obey God's law. He said in Matthew 7:13-14:

> *"If you, then, though you are evil, know how to give good gifts to your children, how much more will your Father in heaven give good gifts to those who ask him! So in everything, do to others what you would have them do to you, for this sums up the Law and the Prophets."*

But, because we're evil, He goes on to let us know that it is not by our obedience to Jewish law alone:

> *"Enter through the narrow gate. For wide is the gate and broad is the way that leads to destruction, and many enter through it. But small is the gate and narrow the way that leads to life, and only a few find it."*

Knowing that it's narrow should motivate us to strive toward the highest possible moral standards and why we need a Savior regardless.

THERE ARE ONLY TWO DESTINATIONS

There's the wide path that leads to eternal destruction, torment, and shame, and the narrow path that leads to eternal life, glory, and honor. In Romans 2:3-8 Paul says,

> "Do you think you will escape God's judgment? Or do you show contempt for the riches of his kindness, forbearance and patience, not realizing that God's kindness is intended to lead you to repentance? But because of your stubbornness and your unrepentant heart, you are storing up wrath against yourself for the day of God's wrath, when his righteous judgment will be revealed. God "will repay each person according to what they have done." To those who by persistence in doing good seek glory, honor and immortality, he will give eternal life. But for those who are self-seeking and who reject the truth and follow evil, there will be wrath and anger."

The Bible always connects both faith in Jesus, a desire for lasting righteousness, and a pursuit of righteousness with life itself. In John 5:22-29 Jesus said,

> "The Father... entrusted all judgment to the Son, that all may honor the Son just as they honor the Father... whoever hears my word and believes him who sent me has eternal life and will not be judged but has crossed over from death to life... a time is coming when all who are in their graves will hear his voice and come out—those who have done what is good will rise to live, and those who have done what is evil will rise to be condemned."

THE WAY TO CHANGE ETERNAL DIRECTIONS

In John 14:6 Jesus said,

> "I am the way and the truth and the life. No one comes to the Father

except through me."

In John 3:36 He also said,

"Whoever believes in the Son has eternal life, but whoever rejects the Son will not see life, for God's wrath remains on them."

In Ephesians 2:7-9 it says that the reason we're saved by faith in Jesus is so that God could,

"Show the incomparable riches of his grace, expressed in his kindness to us in Christ Jesus. For it is by grace you have been saved, through faith—and this is not from yourselves, it is the gift of God—not by works, so that no one can boast."

There are so-called Christians who may have belief in Jesus but not a faith that saves them because they have no desire for righteousness. In Matthew 7:21-23 Jesus said,

"Not everyone who says to Me, 'Lord, Lord,' will enter the kingdom of heaven, but only he who does the will of My Father in heaven. Many will say to Me on that day, 'Lord, Lord, did we not prophesy in Your name, and in Your name drive out demons and perform many miracles?' Then I will tell them plainly, 'I never knew you; depart from Me, you workers of lawlessness!'"

It's not about belief in Jesus alone, but knowing Him and being known by Him, because if you desire this you'll be born again by the Holy Spirit to do the will of the Father.

We're saved by God's grace alone, received by repentance and faith

DAY 1 - WHERE IS YOUR LIFE GOING?

alone, in Christ alone, but not by possessing a faith that is alone. Your good works won't make you good enough or save you but they are evidence of the right kind of faith. Saving faith is evidenced by good works, obedience to God's moral law, righteousness, holiness, love of God and neighbor, and Christ's commands to love one another, preach the gospel and make disciples.

So that's it. You were created and saved to have eternal life with God and glorify Him forever. Your journey will still be difficult, but at least now you have less confusion and distraction about what to do with your life and where you're going. You know the exact direction to go in, how to start today, and how to stay the course until you reach the final destination.

PRAYER

Heavenly Father, I repent of all my sin. I believe Jesus died for my sins and rose from the dead. Fill me with Your Spirit. Thank you for eternal life. Help me live righteous. In Jesus' name. Amen.

JOURNAL

1. Finish this thought: I am saved by _____ because _____. Unpack what this means and explain how salvation works in your own words.

2. Are you on your way to Heaven? How can you be sure? Talk to God about it. Ask Him to help you remember key decisions, defining moments, and the practical ways you live out your faith that confirm your destination.

3. What's the purpose of your life?

Day 2

The Empowered Christian Road Map (Your Life Blueprint)

For a successful life you need to define and pursue success God's way, not the world's way. How can you measure progress? Use this memorable metaphorical biblical blueprint called The Empowered Christian Road Map. Live according to these eight key principles and have unswerving faith, laser-focused direction, and a transformed life driven by purpose and action.

Over the next 28 days you will learn about each part of this framework in greater detail. But for now, reflect on the principles, and in particular, their order. They're already in the best order to know which to focus on first. Which have you been focusing on?

PRINCIPLE #1 - YOU NEED THE RIGHT ROAD MAP

People often assume whatever they've been doing with their lives will eventually bring them happiness and fulfillment, so they just keep chasing the same idols harder. But it doesn't matter how much progress you're making or how many "things" you've accumulated on the way if you've been going in the wrong direction!

To end up at the right destination you need the right road map for your journey. You need to zoom way out and see the big picture. If you don't know where you're starting from, and where you're going, it will make the middle part—life—that much more difficult. But when we view life in this simplistic way it really helps to make a lot of sense out of everything else. It's all about perspective.

The Bible teaches that there's only one true God and He created everything else for His glory. Only the things that bring Him glory with their existence, and also wants the same outcome that He wants in the end, will share in that glorious future with Him.

There's only two final destinations: eternal death and separation from God in Hell, or eternal life as part of God's family with Jesus as Lord and King. Every other principle hinges on this one. Whatever you do with your life needs to be done according to the right road map that leads you to eternal life with Jesus.

Start with your focus here and view the other principles, and everything else in your life, in light of this.

Optional Journal Question: Have you been eternally-minded with your perspective or have you focused on the current situations you're in?

PRINCIPLE #2 - BE REBUILT AND GO IN NEW DIRECTION

In this road map metaphor you're a car and your life is one long journey towards your final destination, which is eternal life with Jesus.

But don't think your journey started when you were born. Yes, everything that happened prior did contribute to you making the decision to follow Jesus, but until you did, you were still under God's wrath and still headed towards the bad destination.

Your journey starts with you being saved and spiritually born again. In other words, you need to be a rebuilt car first. The Holy Spirit must become your driver. He gives you the ability to begin your journey, guarantees you'll make it to the destination, and helps your actions align with the map.

God causes the new birth when we genuinely repent, turn away from our sin, trust in Jesus and the gospel, and make the decision to follow Him.

Optional Journal Question: Describe why you're confident you've done this and God has made you a new creation.

PRINCIPLE #3 - YOU MUST DUMP THE GARBAGE BAGGAGE

You may be a rebuilt car but that doesn't mean you don't have garbage baggage in the car that will hinder your journey. You need to continually examine yourself, making sure that the Holy Spirit is driving and there aren't other bad drivers. You also must remove any bad passengers and ensure that all car doors are closed and locked.

You want to make sure that you're being led by the Holy Spirit and are not being influenced by demonic sources, sinful desires, or lies from culture. You also want to make sure that your journey's direction or progress are not being hindered by unforgiveness, unhealed emotional brokenness, limiting beliefs, toxic relationships, etc.

Continual examination of your vehicle ensures that you're truly rebuilt, that your mind is being renewed, and that your heart and life are being sanctified.

Optional Journal Question: Is there garbage baggage causing hindrances in your life?

PRINCIPLE #4 - CONTROL THE ATMOSPHERE IN THE CAR

Your journey is long with plenty of unpleasant bumps in the road along the way. There's even hazardous obstacles tempting you to turn around and take the smooth journey back. Even if you're unwilling to go back, there's tempting billboards for pleasant distractions and complacency at each exit off ramp.

Jesus did not promise that the journey will be easy, just worth it. Following Jesus is a challenge mentally, physically, and emotionally.

There are many things you can't control on the journey. You can't control what happens outside the car, but you can control the vibe (the thoughts, beliefs, and feelings) inside.

What thoughts do you focus on? What type of messages do you listen to on the radio? What's the internal conversation like in the car? What emotions do you work hard to feel and reflect to those around you? You must do this if you want a vastly more fulfilling and enjoyable journey!

Optional Journal Question: What harmful thoughts, beliefs, and emotions do you experience on a regular basis? What is the cause of them?

PRINCIPLE #5 - THE NEW DIRECTION WILL BE FRUITFUL

During your journey you'll need a compass for navigation. This helps ensure that you're always going in the right direction.

The compass for the Christian life is the fruitfulness of your decisions and actions. Fruitfulness is not just being nice or helping others. It's not defined by what the world calls good, but what God does. Fruitfulness is everything that is an expression of God's character, righteousness, biblical justice, and works of discipleship built on Jesus, our vine.

Fruitfulness begins from the inside-out, prioritizing first your inward transformation, Christlikeness, and character development, then flows out to the external - to your marriage, family, church, and broader community.

Optional Journal Question: Is your life consistently bearing good fruit? If there are areas of bad fruit, have you been prioritizing what God calls good and seeking His help and guidance in those areas?

PRINCIPLE #6 - YOU MUST BE MISSION-PURPOSE DRIVEN

As a follower of Jesus you have an eternal-minded and gospel-centered mission and purpose. All your missional efforts are good fruit, but not everything that is good fruit is part of your mission.

You exist to—and therefor your mission is—to be an ambassador for Christ, preach the gospel, make disciples of Jesus, and build, purify, and edify His bride, the Church.

You exist to be a light in a dark world, confronting sin with righteousness and demonic lies with biblical truth. Your responsibility and privilege is to dispel the forces and influence of Satan in the world to advance the Kingdom of God in those places. And this doesn't change until the end of your race.

Optional Journal Question: Have you been focused and intentional on this purpose and mission? Ask God to help you understand what hindered you from fully embracing this.

PRINCIPLE #7 - PARTNER WITH THE AUTO CLUB

You're not an isolated vehicle lost in the wilderness. You're part of the Auto Club: the Global Church. This is the Body of Christ: the invisible, global collection of all children adopted by God the Father, who've been born again by the Holy Spirit.

You're to be global Church-minded while grounding yourself and focusing the majority of your time, talent, and treasure building up one another within in your local church congregation. And where you will best find your place is within a local church that you're a full, supporting, serving member.

You're to partner with others, united in a common Spirit and mission, serving one another in love. You're to be a community for fellowship, mutual support, sacraments, worship, prayer, preaching, study of God's Word, community outreach and service, evangelism, discipleship, and advancement of God's Kingdom.

Local church congregation involvement isn't optional. It's commanded in Scripture. It's God's design, and it's not a, but the plan, for revival in the world. It's also where you will most utilize your spiritual gifts and calling.

Optional Journal Question: Are you globally Church-minded and fully active member in a local church? If not, what excuses are you believing and giving?

DAY 2 - THE EMPOWERED CHRISTIAN ROAD MAP (YOUR LIFE BLUEPRINT)

PRINCIPLE #8 - SAME DESTINATION, ALTERNATE ROUTES

There is much you'll have in common with other travelers on your journey. You will all be in rebuilt cars by the same manufacturer and have the same driver. You will all be partnered in the same primary mission together, and driving in the same fruitful direction towards the same destination together.

However, you're going to have your own unique testimony, identity, and calling in the Body of Christ as well. You're going to take an alternate route that will have similarities, but it won't be identical to, anyone else's.

You are to discover your highest values, passions, and spiritual gifts, and optimize your personality and talents. You will get the most fulfilling life striving to reach your highest potential developing and pursuing your unique vision and mission.

Optional Journal Question: What is your unique identity, purpose and calling are? Ask God to begin revealing to you what makes you unique and what you are passionate about.

Your journey will still be difficult, but the map shouldn't be! Remember these eight principles as guide posts and use them to monitor your own personal progress throughout your Christian journey, so you can make adjustments as needed. In part two we'll further examine each principle more closely.

PRAYER

Heavenly Father, cement these 8 principles in my memory. Help me live according to them. Help me fix my eyes on Jesus and run this race with wisdom and perseverance! In Jesus' name. Amen.

JOURNAL

Pick at least three of the journal questions and discuss them with God.

Day 3

What's the Purpose of Life?

To know where you are now, and how to get to the right destination, you need an accurate map. What's the purpose of your life? Well, it can be anything, whatever you decide to live for. The Bible calls these things idols. But what's the purpose of life? Why does anything exist at all? What were we created for? For the answer to this, we need to consult with the Creator of life.

GOD CREATED EVERYTHING FOR HIS GLORY

There's only one true God. He's eternal, had no origin, and has always been God. He's all-knowing, all-powerful, and all-present. He's perfect, good, holy, loving, and just. He's not the universe; He's its creator. He's not just a higher power. He's the originator and sustainer of every other power.

He has identity and personality and is relational and knowable. The reason we have these attributes is because He created us like Him in these ways. The universe and everything in it, every galaxy, solar system, sun, planet, animal, plant, cell, and atom proclaims the glory of God. They proclaim His glory in their existence, the same way that a painting's existence proclaims the glory of its painter.

Everything was created by Him and for Him. Why would you want to start a business, family, skill, hobby, or any activity? If you didn't have to do it, why would you? For example, why would you paint a painting? You'd do it because you want to, for your own pleasure, right? It would be an expression and reflection of you. An expression of your thoughts and feelings and a reflection of your talent, creativity, skill, and effort.

Your painting would never be more intrinsically valuable than you are. Its existence proceeds from you. It is the result of your intrinsic value and desire to produce it. And if you were God, and had a limitless reality, you also have the ability to create even more of them. This is why worshipping any created thing, over the creator, is both insulting to God and foolish.

GOD CREATED BEINGS TO KNOW, CELEBRATE, AND SHARE IN HIS GLORY

All of creation is an expression of God for His glory, including angels and humans. He didn't create us to be automatons, mindless and heartless robots that praise Him. He created us intelligent, emotional, spiritual beings able to understand and relate to His attributes.

God is love (1 John 4:16), so He gave us the capability of knowing and loving Him and being known and loved by Him. His most important command, found in Mark 12:30, was:

> *"Love the Lord your God with all your heart and with all your soul and with all your mind and with all your strength."*

But love isn't possible without free will. And if beings are truly and freely capable of love then there's also a potential downside: they could love themselves, or His creation, more than Him, or even choose to hate. Love of ourselves is the root of all idolatry and sin. And hate is also essentially the result of misplaced love given to something else.

After the fall, God's once-beautiful paintings became something ugly, no longer an accurate expression of Him. No longer rightly representing His attributes, likeness, and will to the rest of creation.

Sentient beings like angels and humans also have greater purpose and potential to bring Him glory or disgust in another way. We've been given creative capacity of our own. Unfortunately, we use this greater capacity for evil. Just as a nuclear bomb requires much more skill, intelligence, and ingenuity than a spear does. The very abilities that give us the potential for great good to build up, also give us the potential for great evil to destroy.

The greater your painting represents the best of you, the more glory and joy it gives you. But the more it represents the things you hate, the more disgust it gives you. Would you take a disgusting painting and hang it prominently in the center of your living room forever? Of course not. If some beings God created are like an awful painting why would God allow them to exist so He has to look at it forever? He wouldn't. And He isn't going to.

GOD WILL BE GLORIFIED THROUGH ALL OF THIS

Now you understand the predicament we're all in and what caused it. Let's turn now to why God, who is all-knowing and can see eternity future and know all this would happen, still chose to create us and allow it to.

First, God is glorified through the demonstration of His justice, the reward for good, the punishment for bad, and the destruction of evil. This does express truths about Him. This is why He destroyed most of humanity in a worldwide flood, and later judged Sodom, Egypt, and Canaan. It's why there will be a Judgment Day and Hell as eternal punishment for wicked angels and humans.

Second, God is glorified through the demonstration of His lovingkindness, mercy, and patience. This is the reason He's allowed many to exist at all, and the only thing preventing the immediate and permanent destruction of many people. It's an expression of who He is to extend the time and opportunity to sinners to repent and be saved. He cannot wait forever, but He will patiently wait until the maximum number of all who will turn from their evil, do.

Third, God is glorified through the demonstration of His own love and grace, revealed to lost, sinful prodigal sons and daughters, through His own personal sacrifice on the cross, on their behalf. The gospel reveals the character and heart of God in general, and to the object of His affections: those being saved by it. Though it did take sin to make the gospel possible God has utilized to share the best part of Him with us. This ultimately playing an important role in our free will decision to love Him and desire to spend eternity with Him.

Fourth, God is glorified through the salvation and restoration process. Herein He rescues undeserving bad paintings about to be thrown in the fire and graciously transforms them into good paintings that live and glorify Him forever. He's not pleased by the loss of even a single life, but desires that all would repent and live. (2 Peter 3:9). It's the preference and joy of the Father to save. See the parables of the Lost Sheep, Lost Coin, and Prodigal Son (Luke 15). But in the final analysis, everything will bring Him glory, either through its destruction or its salvation and restoration.

WE'RE INVITED TO BE GOD'S FAMILY FOR ETERNITY

The fifth way God is glorified is having created beings that worship Him and acknowledge that there's nothing greater than He is. That there's nothing more beautiful, loving, or worthy of praise. That there's nothing He has created that is greater than the Creator. That no painting is greater than its painter.

He's glorified by us worshipping Him and being overjoyed at the opportunity to know and love Him forever as our God, family, and highest reward. Pastor John Piper calls this Christian hedonism, saying:

> *"God is most glorified in us when we are most satisfied in Him."* [1]

Understanding the Holy Trinity also brings us into deeper intimacy with God. Jesus reveals the true heart of the Father to us. Hebrews 1:1-3 says,

> *"In the past God spoke... through the prophets... but in these last days he has spoken to us by his Son... The Son is the radiance of God's glory and the exact representation of his being."*

When we're saved, we're baptized into the Son, and we receive the Holy Spirit. In Christ, God the Father adopts us into His family that so He's our father, too. And we all become spiritual brothers and sisters. The Father, Son, and Holy Spirit have been engaging in a type of beautiful dance for all eternity. Through Jesus and the gospel we're invited to join in the dance.

PRAYER

LORD God, everything is for Your glory. May I be a painting that You're pleased with. I'm most satisfied in You. Thank You for knowing and loving me forever. In Jesus' name. Amen.

JOURNAL

1. Ask God to share with you His heart about these things.

2. Ask God how He has been glorified through your testimony and life story. Ask Him to remind you of where you were and how far you've come.

3. Ask the Holy Spirit to reveal to you new ways you could glorify God today. What should you say and to whom? What action should you take?

Day 4

You've been given an Incredible Opportunity

I've got news. You've been given an invitation to an incredible, life changing opportunity! Let me ask you this - would you do walk on hot coals for 6 seconds if I gave you a billion dollars, your dream spouse, and happiness for the rest of your life afterwards? Would you endure that relatively-small sacrifice and temporary discomfort now, in order to receive such a long-lasting reward after? I definitely would!

Jesus promised an even greater reward: to intimately know the creator of all that is good, have absolute total fulfillment, and eternal life. It did take His death for you, but He did that part already. If you want to receive His reward you can have it, just believe that He will give it to you, trust His way, and follow Him over the coals.

GOD DESIGNED BEINGS FOR THIS ETERNAL OPPORTUNITY

God created sentient beings in His image and likeness capable of having an eternal relationship with Him. He did this in two ways.

First, likely because He's a Holy Trinity (three co-eternal and co-equal persons), He made us tripartite (existing with three natures). They are body, soul, and spirit. Put in a more biblically accurate way: you are a soul, united with spirit and a body (1 Thessalonians 5:23).

You don't have a soul; you are a soul: a living, individuated self with intellect, emotion, personality, talents, and creative capacity. Your body is just the physical encasement of your soul and spirit. You still exist without it. Even though the body is good, it's also weak and sin-prone. However, in the resurrection we all get an upgraded, sinless, eternal body.

Your spirit nature is the part of you that is most like God since He is spirit (John 4:24). Your spirit nature is where your conscience is, which is the moral law of God written on the human heart. Your spirit nature enables you to have spiritual connection with God, and be able to house His spiritual presence inside of you.

The second way God designed us for relationship is by creating us with the ability to understand, discern, and love truth. This is an aspect of our free will. Just as we can freely choose to love or hate God, we can freely choose to love or hate truth. We have the ability to reject truth, to try to be our own god, and to worship and live for other created things (Romans 1:18-25).

It's our love of ourselves, desire to worship ourselves, and love of wickedness, that causes us to suppress the truth about God, reality, ourselves, morality, and the purpose of our lives. But our love of, desire for, and capacity for truth, will determine our ultimate eternal destination. The truth is that we were created by God, for God, to be with God. This is where our highest fulfillment, meaning, and purpose will be found. John 14:6 Jesus said,

> *"I am the way and the truth and the life."*

And in John 18:37 He said,

> *"The reason I... came into the world is to testify to the truth. Everyone on the side of truth listens to me."*

God designed us for eternal purpose and put in us everything we need

DAY 4 - YOU'VE BEEN GIVEN AN INCREDIBLE OPPORTUNITY

to respond to this eternal opportunity.

GOD'S "COAL CHALLENGE" TESTS OUR TRUE DESIRES

God could've ensured that humans never had an option to eat the forbidden fruit. But our free will was necessary for genuine love relationship. There's also another good reason He allowed it. The Fall helps us "know" (or experience) evil, but still have the opportunity to love and choose that which is good.

Remember, God wants us to be like Him and want what He wants. So, God didn't cause sin to happen, but He did allow sin to happen, and then use it for the ultimate long term good for many people.

We are saved by trusting the gospel that Jesus died for our sins and living a life consistent with that. When we love God, goodness, and truth, we'll recognize the evil and brokenness in ourselves and others. Our heart will weep at the suffering in the world. Our conscience will be convicted by God's law and want the solution to evil. The result: we'll be overjoyed to hear the gospel!

All of these things come together to draws us to repent of sin, faith in Jesus, and a desire to follow Him, even over hot coals! Our willingness to obey Jesus, and endure trials as result of this decision, is evidence of our trust in Him and our desire of the reward and outcome He's offering. If a person says they have faith, but won't repent of their sins, or follow Him over the coals, then they may have some belief, but they don't have the kind of faith that saves.

As difficult as life in a fallen world is, it's still a gift from God, used to reveal, who we truly are, as well as who He is, in the process. Through the Fall and the gospel we can better appreciate all God's goodness. We can also choose what we want for eternity, who we want to spend it with, and who we want to become in the meantime. Romans 2:7-8 says,

> "To those who by persistence in doing good seek glory, honor and immortality, he will give eternal life. But for those who are self-seeking and who reject the truth and follow evil, there will be wrath and anger."

So... do your actions reflect that you love goodness and truth?

CHRISTIAN LIFE REVEALS WHAT YOU'RE GOING TOWARD

1 Corinthians 9:24-25 says,

> *"Run in such a way as to get the prize. Everyone who competes in the games goes into strict training. They do it to get a crown that will not last, but we do it to get a crown that will last forever."*

No one trains and runs fast for a crown they don't believe in. No one denies their own life, picks up their cross, and follows Jesus, which is what He tells us to do in Matthew 16:24-25, unless they also trust who He claimed to be and the eternal rewards He promised.

Prior to Jesus's incarnation, the way to trust in God's ways, and pursue relationship with Him, was primarily to obey His laws. Jesus helps us do this by fulfilling all of the Civil and Ceremonial parts of the law of God. These laws actually foreshadowed Jesus, who is Himself the fulfillment of them.

Jesus also perfectly fulfilled the Moral law for us by being sinless Himself and then paying the penalty for all of our sins. But He didn't do this so we can sin without worry of punishment. God is holy, moral, and just, and that didn't change. He is righteous and He requires us to be righteous. Jesus didn't lower the standard, He raised it! In fact, in Matthew 5:48 Jesus said,

> *"Be perfect, therefore, as your heavenly Father is perfect."*

Jesus fulfilled the law for us, so that in Him we could be dead to sin and become not less, but MORE moral, just, loving, gracious, and godly! By trusting in the gospel, the guilt and shame of our sinful past are cleansed by the blood of Jesus and replaced with peace and joy. By being born again, our hardened and deadened spirit is made alive again with God's law. It is now written in a more permanent way on our heart and able to continually renew our mind.

All this working together to help us be closer with God and become more like God. Thus, being regenerated (born again) begins the process of us becoming who we want to be for eternity.

This doesn't mean we can't be tempted to sin or that we can't stumble. But pressing forward, towards God, and then stumbling on a sin, is not the same thing as running hard and fast in the wrong direction towards sin.

A person either has the new heart and mind, or they don't. You're either dead to your sin, and crucifying all desire to sin, or you're not dead to sin, resisting it with all your strength, and making excuses. God wants you to be like Him, but you have to want it too. Do you consent to the loss of your ability to sin?

PRAYER

Heavenly Father, I want to spend eternity with You. Jesus, my Lord; I want to become like You. Holy Spirit, I give You consent to remove every sinful desire in me. In Jesus' name. Amen.

JOURNAL

1. Talk to God about your history with sin. What have you struggled with the most and found most difficult to crucify?

2. What is it that you love about those sins? What does it promise and does it deliver on it? Ask God to reveal how He's so much greater of a reward.

3. Do you want to live forever in God's presence? Do you consent to the loss of your ability to sin against Him? Ask Him to help you see it the way He does, to make you hate it the way you should, and deliver you from it.

Day 5

A Final Destination Worth Striving Toward

In Luke 13:23 someone asked if only a few would be saved. Jesus responded,

> "STRIVE to enter through the narrow door. For many, I tell you, will seek to enter and will not be able." They will, "will stand outside knocking and pleading, 'Sir, open the door for us.'... "But he will reply, 'I don't know you or where you come from. Away from me, all you evildoers!' "There will be weeping there, and gnashing of teeth, when you see Abraham, Isaac and Jacob and all the prophets in the kingdom of God, but you yourselves thrown out. People will come from east and west and north and south, and will take their places at the feast in the kingdom of God." (ESV)

This lesson covers: 1) destination #1: Hell, 2) destination #2: Heaven, and 3) eternal life with God is a destination worth striving toward.

DESTINATION #1: HELL (ETERNAL DEATH, SEPARATION FROM GOD, AND TORMENT)

The Bible severely and repeatedly warns about Hell, a place sinners will go to forever when they die. It's described as eternal conscious torment, "outer darkness," for "eternal punishment, shame and everlasting contempt, where there will be weeping and gnashing of teeth," and they, "will be tormented day and night for ever and ever." (Matt. 8:12, 13:41-50, 25:30-46; Dan. 12:2; Rev. 20:10).

But it's also described as a place of "everlasting destruction" (2 Thess. 1:9) through consumption often associated with fire. It's called "the lake of fire," "the fiery furnace," the "fiery lake of burning sulfur," and "where the fire is never quenched," (Mark 9:48; Rev. 20:15). In Matthew 10:28 Jesus said,

"Do not be afraid of those who kill the body but cannot kill the soul. Instead, be afraid of the One who can destroy both soul and body in hell."

Jesus warned if your eye or hand causes you to sin it would be better to pluck it out and cut it off than for your whole body to be thrown into Hell (Matt. 5:29-30). But isn't God good, loving and merciful? Yes, but He's also a just judge. A judge that says to a child molester "you can go free, because I'm good and merciful" is NOT a good judge! He's depraved and corrupt. That would be a perversion of justice and hatred towards the molester's victims.

Thus, it's God's goodness that requires evil be punished in Hell. We all agree Hitler, terrorists, molesters, etc. deserve Hell. But God's standards are higher than ours so we're all sinners. We've sinned against ourselves, others, and creation. We've sinned against God even though He gives us life itself, and every single breath, heartbeat, and good thing we've ever experienced.

Wanting people to simply cease existing, with no reward of eternal life but no consequences for an evil life, is an unjust evil desire. God is both loving and just—both merciful and wrathful. Not either/or.

The cross shows us this best. On it, we see the intersection of perfect love and perfect justice. The feeling of rejection from God, public shame, and agonizing execution for sins, that's perfect justice. The perfect, sinless Son of God, volunteering to be mocked, suffer, killed, and feeling His Father turn His eyes from Him for the first time in all of eternity—just to pay the penalty for guilty sinners that He loves—that's perfect love.

DESTINATION #2: HEAVEN (ETERNAL LIFE WITH GOD AND GLORY)

When it comes to what motivates us, sometimes we need the stick, sometimes the carrot. God warns us about Hell so we fear it and repent, that's the stick. But He also provides the carrot. He tells how amazing the alternative is. Heaven on a future New Earth, living in resurrected eternal bodies, perfect relationship with God, and no curse, sin, sorrow, or death! Revelation 21:3-7 says,

> *"God's dwelling place is now among the people... 'He will wipe every tear from their eyes. There will be no more death' or mourning or crying or pain, for the old order of things has passed away... Those who are victorious will inherit all this, and I will be their God and they will be my children."*

We run towards the joy of, "living in God's presence," "seeing God face to face," when "we shall be like Him, because we shall see Him as He is." (Ps. 140:13; Matt. 5:8; Rev. 22:4; 1 John 3:2). He tells us to run towards the "Paradise of God" (Rev. 2:7), "fullness of joy," and "pleasures forevermore," where we "feast on the abundance of His house," and "drink from the river of His delights." (Ps. 16:11, 36:8). How awesome does that sound?!

We run towards eternal rewards like the crown of glory that will never fade away (1 Pet. 5:4), the crown of life God promises to those who love Him (Jam. 1:12), and the crown of righteousness for all who have longed for the Lord's appearing (2 Tim. 4:8). The crowns we race toward are imperishable, undefiled, unfading ones, already reserved in Heaven for us (1 Pet. 1:4). Strive towards the victory of accomplishment, and the right to sit with Jesus on His throne, just as He overcame and sat down with His Father on His throne! (Rev. 3:21). Then we will shine like the brightness of the heavens, shining like the stars forever (Dan. 12:3).

Heaven will not be a bunch of winged angel babies playing harps on clouds! That is so unbiblical. Picture having an abundance of every good thing about this world, yet, without sin, death, and demons negatively affecting it. And above that, whatever good new gifts God has in store for us, His children! Trust that God knows exactly how to create a Paradise. Whatever good things you enjoy about this fallen world are NOTHING compared to the life to come so persevere and run the race towards it!

LIFE WITH GOD IS A DESTINATION WORTH STRIVING TOWARD

God doesn't want anyone to go to Hell, but all to repent (2 Pet. 3:9). But He won't allow you to waver between two options forever. He gives us this life to decide what we want to be, which determines where we will go. If we use this life to show Him in every possible way we reject the gospel, don't want to spend time with God, doing things that glorify God, He's is not going to force us to for eternity.

We need the fear of God and the love for God! This is the beginning of wisdom (Prov. 9:10). 2 Cor. 7:1 says,

> *"Therefore, since we have these promises ... let us purify ourselves from everything that contaminates body and spirit, perfecting holiness out of reverence for God."*

The final destination of everyone being saved is to be a child of God the Father. Show that you believe and want this by living as His child right now. The final destination is to become like Jesus. Show that you want this by striving to be like Him now. Your closeness to God is dependent upon how much time you invest in your relationship with Him! Revelation 17:14 says,

> *"the Lamb will triumph over them because he is Lord of lords and King of kings—and with him will be his called, chosen and faithful followers."*

Be one of these followers and strive on towards the destination, knowing that you will have victory!

PRAYER

Heavenly Father, give me wisdom to fear You, Hell, and eternal separation from You. Set eternity in my heart and help me strive toward glorious eternal life with You. In Jesus' name. Amen.

JOURNAL

1. Talk to God about what you think Hell will be like. Describe what comes to your mind as you meditate on how it's described in the Bible. What would be the worst part of it?

2. Talk to God about what you think Heaven will be like. Describe what comes to your mind as you meditate on how it's described in the Bible. What would be the best part of it that you're looking forward to?

3. Ask the Lord who you could talk about this with today. You could just tell them it was something you read earlier so it's still on your mind. Are they saved already? If not, do they fear God and love God? Ask them what motivates them more, the carrot or the stick?

Day 6

Why you Must be Born Again to be Saved

Unlike most religions, Christianity isn't about just believing the right things and doing the right activities. To receive salvation, God must miraculously intervene and cause us to be supernaturally born again. This new birth is absolutely necessary. This lesson explains why.

YOU'VE GOT A BAD MAP

You need to be born again to replace the map you were born with that's leading you to Hell. False religion say humans are generally good but Ecclesiastes 7:20 says,

> *"There is no one on earth who is righteous, no one who does what is right and never sins."*

Romans 3:10-12 says,

> *"There is no one righteous, not even one; there is no one who understands; there is no one who seeks God. All have turned away, they have together become worthless; there is no one who does good, not even one."*

How we navigate the world, what seems good to us as the way to live and what to live for is, by God's standards, often evil. Ephesians 2:1-3 says,

> *"You were dead in your transgressions and sins, in which you used to live when you followed the ways of this world and of... the spirit... at work in those who are disobedient. All of us also... gratifying the cravings of our flesh and following its desires and thoughts. Like the rest, we were by nature deserving of wrath."*

Romans 3:23 states,

> *"All have sinned and fall short of the glory of God."*

We're not good; we deserve God's wrath. Even when we try to obey God's law to do good we inevitably still fall short of God's standards. Jesus finished His Sermon on the Mount in Matthew 5:48 saying, "Be perfect, therefore, as your heavenly Father is perfect."

Apart from Jesus you are not innocent before God. You're not only still guilty of all outward sins you've committed, you're also guilty of the wicked inner thoughts and desires of the heart you secretly enjoy. Romans 3:9, 20 says,

> *"Jews and Gentiles alike are all under the power of sin... no one will be declared righteous in God's sight by the works of the law; rather, through the law we become conscious of our sin."*

YOU'VE GOT A BROKEN CAR

Another problem is your own nature. You are the car for the journey: your body, mind, spirit, emotions, desires. This is the vehicle you travel through life in. But God says you need more than a tune-up, you need a new vehicle. The curse of sin and death began with the sin of Adam and Eve in the Garden of Eden (Gen. 3:16-19). Romans 5:12 says,

> *"Just as sin entered the world through one man, and death through sin, and in this way death came to all people, because all sinned."*

Since this first generation the effects have compounded like compound interest in the bank getting worse. These are the doctrines of "original sin" and "human depravity." Think you're not a sinner? 1 John 1:8 says,

> *"If we claim to be without sin, we deceive ourselves and the truth is not in us."*

Psalm 51:5 King David said,

> *"Surely I was sinful at birth, sinful from the time my mother conceived me."*

You were born that way. We inherited this sin nature that's corrupted by, and inclined to, sin. Romans 1 describes how our consciences testify this, but we suppress it to pursue our unrighteous desires.

To recognize your depravity, notice the struggle within to do good. This is why there's a struggle and a choice to do good, because parts of us don't want to! If we were truly good we'd just do what's right and not have to choose to.

The sin nature includes with it the consequences of sin, such as toil, pain, death, and decay. Sin is all-consuming like a cancer that has spread to every cell of our body. God's Word says we're depraved, broken, and sick, and if we're humble enough to realize, acknowledge, and confess this to ourselves and God, He'll heal us.

Romans 6 describes that since the sin nature is still a part of us, even after being born again, we must intentionally choose to crucify it daily. Don't be self-righteous and deny this. Be humble enough to accept it so you can turn to Jesus, the Great Physician!

YOU'VE GOT POOR EYESIGHT

How we see ourselves and others is also negatively affected by our sin nature. Sin causes separation from God's truth. We tend to see ourselves as good and those who disagree with us as bad. Sin deceives and blinds us to see through a skewed, selfish lens. Jesus said to stop being a hypocrite and first remove the log from your own eye so you can see clearly enough to remove the speck from your brother's eye afterwards (Matt. 7:5).

Everyone has a moral code they live by but it's viewed through this kind of sin-distorted perspective. We submit only to certain parts of the law, parts we find comfortable, while condemning others for doing the same. Many religious people condemn others for their sins, while ignoring a different kind of their own. Maybe they condemn homosexual behavior while ignoring their own adultery, fornication, pornography, or lust. Maybe they condemn tobacco, because it's bad for the body, while ignoring their own gluttony, obesity, and stressful living which harms and leads to even more deaths.

If you keep your old nature and eyes, while being religious, it only leads to Pharisaism. When inwardly-spiritually-dead sinners try to muster up the strength to obey God outwardly, while they sin differently, or while they're still desiring sinful things inwardly. Jesus' taught in His parable of the Pharisee and the Tax Collector in Luke 18:9-14,

> "All those who exalt themselves will be humbled, and those who humble themselves will be exalted." (v. 14)

YOU MUST BE BORN AGAIN

John 3:3-6 Jesus said,

> "No one can see the kingdom of God unless they are born again... Flesh gives birth to flesh, but the Spirit gives birth to spirit."

If God hasn't rebuilt your car, given you a new map, new eyes, and become your driver, you'll never get to the desired destination. All have a sin nature, love sin, and have an inclination to continue to sin. So we all need to be born again and empowered by the Spirit to kill that sin nature daily.

If we're not, we'll be a miserable replica going through the motions.

DAY 6 - WHY YOU MUST BE BORN AGAIN TO BE SAVED

Maybe doing the same religious activities, but never with peace, joy, contentment, from the Holy Spirit or lasting victory over sin. Galatians 6:15 says,

> *"Neither circumcision nor uncircumcision means anything; what counts is the new creation."*

You can't decide to be born or to assist in your spiritual birth. All you can do is throw out the old map, die to the old way, repent of your sins, humble yourself before God, and surrender your life wholly to Jesus. If you stumble on sin later, reaffirm your repentance and your faith in the gospel. We never outgrow the gospel. We only mature in our understanding of just how dependent we are on it. Pursue a life of continuously growing in your new nature.

PRAYER

Heavenly Father, I repent of all my sins. Make me a new creation. Remove all sinful desire in me. Cleanse me of all sin and empower me to walk in victory over every sin. In Jesus' name. Amen.

JOURNAL

1. Why must be spiritually born again from above? Why is this necessary and why do you think God set it up to work this way?

2. What kinds of things would you look for as evidence of a person claiming to be a Christian but not born again yet? How might a person's attitudes and behaviors be seen by outsiders as to "what Christians are like"?

3. Ask God to highlight someone to you that claims to be Christian but may not be born again yet. Discuss ways to bring this up with them today and help to disciple them.

Day 7

Understanding the Process of Salvation

Yesterday we looked at why we must be born again to be saved. This lesson is about how the process of salvation works. It covers: 1) Everything hinges on God's grace, 2) We must be humble and repent, 3) Justification and imputed righteousness, 4) Salvation is by faith alone.

EVERYTHING HINGES ON GOD'S GRACE

Grace, from the Greek word *charis*, means favor, blessing, or kindness. It's the unmerited favor of God extended to undeserving sinners, given in many ways.

First, God gives everyone a Common Grace (divine providence), restraining sin on earth, providing universal blessings like crops and rain, ordaining civil authorities to maintain order and punish wrong.

Second, God graciously forgives sinners offering us forgiveness, reconciliation, restoration, and glorification. We don't deserve that. God would be perfectly just to allow us to suffer the consequences of our sin. He's not required to pardon us. He doesn't have a moral commitment to provide a way for guilty people to be forgiven. It's by God's grace that any way is available at all. He's glorified by being gracious towards us this way.

Third, God graciously calls us to Himself with a "Prevenient grace" (meaning a grace that precedes or comes beforehand to pave the way). This grace is a supernatural softening of the hardness of our sinful condition. He's actively convicting the world of sin, and righteousness, and drawing us towards our need for Jesus (John 6:37-44, 16:7-11).

Fourth, God graciously provides the Savior who did all that was needed for every person to be saved, sending the gospel message out far and wide. He also enabled us to be responsible (response-able) to His appeals through the "Illuminating grace" of the Gospel and His Word. This can break our stubborn resistance and compel us to respond upon hearing.

Fifth, God graciously preserves all those who are in the process of being saved, continually forgiving our sinful nature, sanctifying and empowering us to endure to the end. Ephesians 2:5-7 says,

> *"It is by grace you have been saved... in order that... he might show the incomparable riches of his grace, expressed in his kindness to us in Christ Jesus."*

BY HUMILITY WE REPENT

Repentance means to see reality and sin differently, stop going toward sin, do a 180 and go in the opposite direction toward God. Before we can repent, believe in Jesus and live obediently, we must be humbled by our undeservedness.

We must see our sinfulness, brokenness, and imperfections in light of God's infinite majesty. When we see ourselves as we truly are, flawed and drenched in uncleanness, we would prostrate ourselves and cry out the way Isaiah did in Isaiah 6:5-7,

> *"Woe to me!" I cried. "I am ruined! For I am a man of unclean lips, and I live among a people of unclean lips, and my eyes have seen the King, the LORD Almighty." (v. 5)*

James 4:6 says,

> "But he gives us more grace. Therefore it says, "God opposes the proud but gives grace to the humble." (ESV)

We're not good, don't deserve, and don't earn, merit, or help our salvation in any way. It's 100% by God's grace. 1 Peter 5:6 says,

> "Humble yourselves, therefore, under God's mighty hand, that he may lift you up in due time."

JUSTIFICATION AND IMPUTED RIGHTEOUSNESS

Justification means to be judicially declared righteous by God. Jesus justifies us through Atonement. I like to remember it as "at-one-ment," because through it we become one with God.

The main thing Jesus accomplished on the cross was Penal Substitutionary Atonement. Jesus paid our sin penalty (penal), by being our substitute, bearing the punishment that we deserve. This is a propitiatory sacrifice meaning it satisfied God's anger and wrath against sin. This is necessary for God to forgive and come into relationship with guilty sinners without lacking justice or compromising His holy standards. Ephesians 1:7-8 says,

> "In Him [Christ] we have redemption through His blood, the forgiveness of our sins, in accordance with the riches of God's grace that he lavished on us."

Another important thing that Jesus accomplished for us on the cross is what I'm calling a modified version of the Ransom Theory.

Sin, and the wages of sin, death, are owed to God. We're in a prison enslaved by sin, and the consequence of sin, death, so we're also enslaved to the one who holds the power of death, Satan. (Rom. 6:22-23; Heb. 2:14).

Jesus offered Himself as a ransom (a liberty-price)—to God—for our freedom from Sin. 1 Timothy 2:5-6 says,

> *"For there is one God and one mediator between God and mankind, the man Christ Jesus, who gave himself as a ransom for all people."*

Acts 20:28 says,

> *"Be shepherds of the church of God, which he bought with his own blood."*

There are other things Jesus accomplished on the cross but they're not as important as the previous two items mentioned above when it comes to our our salvation. He also:

1. Did a reversal of Adam and all humanity's rebellion to God by being completely submissive and obedient, even unto death on a cross.
2. Gave God the honor and glory He was due.
3. Triumphed over sin, death, Hell, and Satan.
4. Modeled submission and obedience to give us a moral example.

Another really great swap that occurred was His Imputed Righteousness. Basically, Jesus also had the consequence of our sins imputed to Him, meaning it was counted or credited to Him, so He received it as though He was guilty. While this happened, His righteousness was imputed to us, making us righteous! 2 Corinthians 5:21 says,

> *"God made Him who knew no sin to be sin on our behalf, so that in Him we might become the righteousness of God."*

Romans 6:18 says,

> *"You have been set free from sin and have become slaves to righteousness."*

BY FAITH ALONE WE'RE SAVED

Romans 3:23-26 connects all of this, saying:

> *"For all have sinned and fall short of the glory of God, and all are justified freely by his grace through the redemption that came by Christ Jesus. God presented Christ as a sacrifice of atonement, i through the shedding of his blood—to be received by faith. He did this to demonstrate his righteousness... so as to be just and the one who justifies those who have faith in Jesus."*

We're saved by our faith in Jesus alone and in no way is this assisted by keeping God's laws or commandments. Romans 10:3-4 says,

> *"Since they did not know the righteousness of God and sought to establish their own, they did not submit to God's righteousness. Christ is the culmination of the law so that there may be righteousness for everyone who believes."*

Salvation is a gift of God's grace. It's essential we do live a righteous life of good works but this is a response to salvation, not something that helps earn/merit it through good works. Ephesians 2:8-10 says,

> *"For it is by grace you have been saved, through faith—and this is not from yourselves, it is the gift of God—not by works, so that no one can boast. For we are God's handiwork, created in Christ Jesus to do good works..."*

The kind of faith that saves is at the intersection of Knowledge, Belief, and Trust. It's not correct beliefs alone. It's also trust in Jesus demonstrated through action. Saving faith always produces outward fruit (good works) as evidence of the inward change of heart, belief, trust, obedience, and commitment.

PRAYER

LORD God, thank You for Your grace and gift of salvation. Help me trust in Jesus' atonement alone, not my works, and be humble, grateful, faithful, obedient, and righteous. In Jesus' name. Amen.

JOURNAL

1. Meditate on these truths and tell God in your own words how thankful you are for His grace that made all of these other things possible.

2. The number one thing besides idolatry and love of self, that keeps a person's heart hard, unrepentant, and resistant to the promptings of the Holy Spirit, is humility. Why do you think this is?

3. Do you struggle with pride? Do you struggle with thinking that you can still someone help Jesus with your salvation? Do you want God to take away all your pride and help you remain humble? Would you be willing to suffer and have a less comfortable and enjoyable life if it was necessary to purify your heart? Talk with God about it.

Day 8

What does it Mean to be a New Creation in Christ?

What happens when we're born again? What does it mean to be a new creation in Christ? Using the metaphor that each person is like a car, and their life like a journey, being a new creation means that we get a new car, new driver, new mechanic, new fuel system, and new owner's manual!

YOU'RE A NEW CAR

Ephesians 2:10 says,

> "For we are God's handiwork, created in Christ Jesus to do good works, which God prepared in advance for us to do."

2 Corinthians 5:17 says,

> "Therefore, if anyone is in Christ, the new creation has come: The old has gone, the new is here!"

You are spirit, soul, and body (1 Thess. 5:23). Your body is the vehicle you get around in, your spirit was made new by the Holy Spirit when you were born again, and your soul is being sanctified by Him.

1 Corinthians 6:19-20 says,

> "Do you not know that your bodies are temples of the Holy Spirit, who is in you, whom you have received from God? You are not your own; you were bought at a price. Therefore honor God with your bodies."

YOU HAVE A NEW DRIVER

This means that you're no longer in the driver seat in control. You've accepted Jesus as Lord and you've agreed to allow the Holy Spirit to lead and guide you. Move over to the passenger seat - He's leading now! John 10:27 Jesus said,

> "My sheep listen to my voice; I know them, and they follow me"

and in John 16:13,

> "When he, the Spirit of truth, comes, he will guide you into all the truth."

The Spirit helps us crucify the sinful desires of the flesh that lead to death and live in a way that glorifies God. Romans 8:6,9 says,

> "The mind governed by the flesh is death, but the mind governed by the Spirit is life and peace... You, however, are not in the realm of the flesh but are in the realm of the Spirit, if indeed the Spirit of God lives in you."

Galatians 5:24-25 says,

> "Those who belong to Christ Jesus have crucified the flesh with its passions and desires. Since we live by the Spirit, let us keep in step with the Spirit."

Submit to Him and be fruitful!

YOU HAVE AN IN-CAR MECHANIC

You no longer have to rely on your own self-improvement effort. Jesus, by the person of the Holy Spirit, is now living in the car with you and He heals, repairs, restores, renews, corrects, and establishes you during the journey. 1 Thessalonians 5:23 says,

> *"May God himself, the God of peace, sanctify you through and through. May your whole spirit, soul and body be kept blameless at the coming of our Lord Jesus Christ. The one who calls you is faithful, and he will do it."*

This includes everything you need: correction of false beliefs, renewing the mind, healing emotional brokenness, deliverance from demons, spiritual growth, and assistance with personal growth. 1 Peter 5:10 says,

"The God of all grace, who has called you to his eternal glory in Christ, after you have suffered a little while, will himself restore you and make you strong, firm and steadfast."

YOU HAVE A NEW FUEL SYSTEM

You've also received a new, supernatural, nuclear powerhouse! You're no longer a 4 cylinder; you're a V12! Acts 1:8 Jesus said,

> *"You will receive power when the Holy Spirit comes on you; and you will be my witnesses."*

Ephesians 1:19-20 Paul says the One who works powerfully within us is has the same mighty strength He exerted when He raised Christ from the dead!

The Holy Spirit also provides the life and fuel for your journey. While you should still honor the Sabbath principle and give yourself rest, you also have within a renewable spiritual energy source within. Lean into

Him and draw help when needed. Colossians 1:29 says,

> "I strenuously contend with all the energy Christ so powerfully works in me."

You can do all things through Christ who gives you strength (Phil. 4:13).

YOU HAVE A NEW OWNER'S MANUAL

Matthew 4:4 Jesus said,

> "It is written: 'Man shall not live on bread alone, but on every word that comes from the mouth of God.'"

Like a car owner's manual, the Bible teaches us how to operate ourselves, how the church should function, and so much more. The Bible is our GPS, weather forecast, shield, and sword against the enemy. The Bible is the God-breathed, Holy Spirit-inspired guide to all that we need to know for faith and life.

The Bible is a collection of 66 different books, poems, and letters, written over a span of 1600 years (from approx. 1500 BC to AD 100), by more than 40 authors all led by God in their writing. As a whole, it consists of key historical events, warnings to humanity to prepare them of God's judgment to come, and an aid to God's people to guide them through perilous times.

It's also a love letter from God to humanity, sharing His heart and affection for us, teaching us the way to true human flourishing, and how to be reconciled to Him. Its compilation into 66 books, transmission down to us over the centuries all the way into modern times, and translations from the original languages are highly documented and trustworthy.

The Bible is the most reliable, foundational source of what to know about God, ultimate truth, salvation, eternal life, and how to practically live out our faith. It's also self-authenticating in a number of ways. 2 Timothy 3:15-16 says,

> *"The Holy Scriptures, which are able to make you wise for salvation through faith in Christ Jesus. All Scripture is God-breathed and is useful for teaching, rebuking, correcting and training in righteousness, so that the servant of God may be thoroughly equipped for every good work."*

The Bible is not just the teachings of humans. It's God's Living Word, inspired by Him. This makes reading, knowing, and trusting it a high octane boost that amplifies the fuel of the Holy Spirit inside of us. The Holy Spirit inspired and preserves His Word. And He loves it when you love it. 2 Peter 1:20-21 says,

> *"You must understand that no prophecy of Scripture came about by the prophet's own interpretation of things. For prophecy never had its origin in the human will, but prophets, though human, spoke from God as they were carried along by the Holy Spirit."*

His Word testifies of its own self-revealing divine authenticity. When we study it—as long as we do with humility, repentance, and faith, in search of Him, godly wisdom and instruction—He meets us there, illuminating His Word to our mind and spirit, giving us understanding.

His Word also simultaneously confirms His presence in us, testifying to the majesty and lordship of Jesus, building us up spiritually, empowering our faith and walk. Hebrews 4:12 says,

> *"For the word of God is alive and active. Sharper than any double-edged sword, it penetrates even to dividing soul and spirit, joints and marrow; it judges the thoughts and attitudes of the heart."*

Summarized best in The Chicago Statement on Biblical Inerrancy, the Bible is without error in its foundation and instructions for faith and life. In ancient times there were no street lights at night. The only way to not trip or fall into a pit was to hold a lamp in front of you as you walked. The

DAY 8 - WHAT DOES IT MEAN TO BE A NEW CREATION IN CHRIST?

Bible does this: it gives us light for direction so we don't fall into a pit. Psalm 119:105 says,

> *"Your word is a lamp for my feet, a light on my path."*

PRAYER

LORD God, thank You for making me a new creation. I will follow You into the Promised Land. Be my mechanic and restore me. Help me to know and trust Your Word. In Jesus' name. Amen.

JOURNAL

1. Which of these areas of being a new creation do you need improvement in the most? (Your identity as a new car, being led by a new driver, letting Him be your mechanic, full use of your new fuel system, or knowledge in and trust of your new owner's manual?) Ask God to reveal this to you and ask Him to help you understand why this is the case.

2. Which of these six areas are you already utilizing the most and very confident in? Ask God to highlight someone in your mind that struggles in that area that He would like you to reach out to today about it.

3. Which of these six areas would you like to grow more in, even if you wouldn't describe yourself as "needing improvement?" Describe why you want more of this for all the right reasons. Spend some time in prayer asking the Father to give you more of the fullness of this in your life beginning with today. Write down His response. If you feel that He has answered yes, do something to test it out.

Day 9

How Satan is the Saboteur of your Journey

Satan, along with sin, is our great spiritual enemy. Despite the caricature he's often portrayed as, he isn't actually adorned in red with horns, hooves, and mustache with a pitchfork in hand.

I'm not sure if it's a good thing we caricature him this way or not. On the plus side, we view him as weaker and insignificant. However, many Christians likely underestimate him as a result. Thus they have terrible defense, even when they're literally having their entire life destroyed by his forces.

As an experienced deliverance minister I can tell you that demons usually hide in the background. They rarely make it known to the host human that they are present and influencing their situation at all. And when they do make their presence known they usually don't admit that they are malevolent.

When people know that spiritual entities are there, their typical strategy is to continue to pretend to be benevolent, or at least neutral and trivial, while continuing to deceive and destroy from within.

2 Corinthians 11:14-15 says,

DAY 9 - HOW SATAN IS THE SABOTEUR OF YOUR JOURNEY

> "Satan himself masquerades as an angel of light. It is not surprising, then, if his servants also masquerade as servants of righteousness."

This lesson, we'll learn who Satan is and how he's a saboteur, as it says in 2 Corinthians 2:11,

> "In order that Satan might not outwit us. For we are not unaware of his schemes."

WHO IS SATAN?

Satan is a cherub, 1 of 3 types of spirit beings God created. The other two are archangels and seraphs. We generally refer to all three types broadly as angels. Like humans, angels were created sentient and blameless, having free will, and the ability to love God and live for His glory, or to love and live for themselves. Satan chose the latter. He wants you to love and prioritize yourself, too.

Isaiah 14:12 he's called "Lucifer," a 4th century Latin translation of a word meaning "Shining One." In Isaiah 14:12-14 Satan said,

> "I will raise my throne above the stars of God... I will make myself like the Most High."

God responded,

> "How you have fallen from heaven, morning star, son of the dawn! [Lucifer] You have been cast down to the earth."

Ezekiel 28:12-17 God says to him,

> "You were the seal of perfection, full of wisdom and perfect in beauty. You were in Eden... You were anointed as a guardian cherub... You were blameless in your ways from the day you were created till wickedness was found in you... Your heart became proud on account of your beauty...

> *you corrupted your wisdom because of your splendor. So I threw you to the earth."*

Satan wants you to have pride that leads to arrogance and wickedness too. Satan led 1/3 of the angels in Heaven in rebellion against God and they were all cast to the spiritual realm on earth with him (Rev. 12:4). This is what demons are: fallen angels, disembodied spirit beings.

The word Satan means "adversary," and the word Devil means "slanderer." He's an adversary and slanderer of both God and us. He wants you to doubt God and believe him when he says that God is bad, untrustworthy, and is holding back from you. He also wants you to believe the opposite about him: that he's the good guy in the story and offers something worthwhile.

What he did in Genesis 3 is exactly what he's still doing today. Whereas Jesus is the way, the truth, and the life (John 14:6), Satan is the reverse. He is "the false way, the lie, and the death" (John 14:6).

Satan is merely a created being and is not all knowing, all powerful, or present in more than one place at a time. Only God is these things. However, Satan (and his demons) love trying to convince people he is all of those things.

There's only one chief Satan. Demons possessing people may claim to be the Satan or Lucifer but statistically almost all of them are not. "Satan" is also a rank in the demonic hierarchy. But from now on, when I say Satan I'm referring to the chief angel, the Satan rank, and all other demons because they basically operate in similar ways.

HOW SATAN IS THE SABOTEUR

A saboteur engages in sabotage, the act of deliberately destroying, damaging, or obstructing something, especially for political or military advantage. Subversion is the systematic attempt to overthrow or undermine a government or political system by working secretly from within. Satan is using subversion to infiltrate individuals, marriages, families, small groups, churches, institutions, governments, politics, media, technologies, etc.

DAY 9 - HOW SATAN IS THE SABOTEUR OF YOUR JOURNEY

His primary means are sin, brokenness, and deception. His common vision is to steal, kill, and destroy (John 10:10). His mission is to overthrow or undermine the healing, deliverance, restoration, or other advancement of the Kingdom of God in those areas.

Satan's external attacks are not always obvious. But most people with internal demons also don't know that they have them because they hide undetected in the background. Sinful flesh, mental illness, bad genetics, poor diet or health, bad habits, poverty, government, politics, other people, etc. get blamed. Satan wins when he can attack you and you have no idea he's even behind the problem.

The sinful world clearly has an influence on believers, but Satan also gets a lot of influence even in the lives of Christians who are not biblically astute, introspective, or spiritually discerning.

Satan has been at this for thousands of years and he's quite good at it! He's rarely in the open, telling you he's Satan, he's evil, he hates you, and exactly how he's destroying you in different aspects of your life. He's rarely going to openly reveal where he's hiding, how long he's been there, how he got access, how he stays there, and how exactly he's actively sabotaging you in that area.

Those demons are not going to tell you that they'd rather put up with staying there and enduring your Christian worship than be a disembodied spirit back in the Abyss and have to report back to Satan that they failed their assignment. They're not going to tell you that they won't leave on their own and won't go unless you identify them, remove their rights to stay, and aggressively force them to leave.

They're not going to tell you that you should be much more concerned with your sanctification and removing all sinful, toxic, ungodly influences from your life because they only increase their stronghold over you. They're not going to tell you that you should prioritize expelling demonic baggage like him because if he stays he's going to keep damaging, sabotaging, and deceiving you with the goal of trying to get you to ultimately reject Jesus and be thrown into Hell with him!

No, he hides in the background skillfully playing the long game. Making you think all your problems are your fault, even reminding you to feel guilt and shame about it. He won't tell you these things—but I will!

Just as a political saboteur can do more damage if they remain undetected and work their way to be president, Satan can do more damage if he works his way up undetected to influence us, or others through us, at higher levels.

Now sometimes in prideful arrogance they blow their cover and overtly attack because they have a stronghold and feel secure that you couldn't remove them even if you tried. Sometimes they even gain increased influence through direct contact, to build trust or get more deeply embedded, often claiming to be good as in the case of angels, spirit guides, or ancestors.

Sometimes demons get flushed to the surface by God so you deal with them. My philosophy is let them get forced to the surface ASAP so that you can expel them once and for all.

EXAMINE YOUR LIFE

1 Peter 5:8-9 says,

> *"Be alert and of sober mind. Your enemy the devil prowls around like a roaring lion looking for someone to devour. Resist him, standing firm in the faith."*

Satan hinders many ways but most important are those that derail your eternal destination by denying essential Christian doctrine, trust in the gospel, and a holy life that glorifies God. The Christian life is a daily denial of the old and an embrace of the new (Luke 9:23-25). Crucify the sinful desires of the flesh daily (Gal. 5:24). Prioritize your sanctification: your spiritual, mental, emotional, and relational health.

PRAYER

Heavenly Father, help me die to my old sinful self and embrace my new identity in Christ. Increase my deliverance knowledge and spiritual discernment to recognize where the enemy is affecting me. Completely deliver, heal, sanctify, and fill me with Your Holy Spirit. In Jesus' name. Amen.

JOURNAL

1. Do you believe what the Bible says about Satan and demons and what they are doing even to Christians? Why do you think many churches and believers believe in the "idea" of Satan but on a practical day-to-day level don't act like it could ever be Satan?

2. What areas of your life could Satan (demons) be sabotaging from behind the scenes? Talk to God about any areas you're not walking in total victory, wholeness, and holiness. Ask Him for discernment and understanding about how Satan could be involved.

3. Take authority against any area of your life still in bondage and command Satan and any demon connected to that area to leave immediately in the name of Jesus. If you feel resistance continue to press in and fight. Talk to God about your experience and ask Him for understanding.

Day 10

The 4 Main Ways Satan leads people to Hell

There are four main ways Satan leads people to Hell. They are:

1. False Religion
2. False Spirituality
3. Carnal Compromise
4. Counterfeit Jesuses

They're all deception-based, with the ultimate goal to prevent people from knowing the true God, trusting the true gospel, or surrendering their lives to the true Jesus. In The Empowered Christian Road Map metaphor you are a car, and your life the journey.

To ensure that you're headed in the right direction toward eternal life, you must secure your car from these four ways being a driver or passenger.

Satan has a stronghold if he has a driver with deep embedment and a secure position controlling your direction. Satan has a foothold if he has a passenger in the car able to influence you at all, even subtly.

Ephesians 4:27 says,

"Do not give the devil a foothold."

2 Corinthians 10:3-4 says,

"For though we live in the world, we do not wage war as the world does. The weapons we fight with are not the weapons of the world. On the contrary, they have divine power to demolish strongholds."

Whether a bad driver or a bad passenger, evict these four from your car!

FALSE RELIGION

This is any religious system that distorts correct understanding of who God is, or any religious practice that distorts the correct way to reconcile your relationship with the true God.

The philosophy here is Legalism. Examples include Islam, Modern Judaism, Roman Catholicism, and Shinto. Some recognize that there's a God; a problem with evil, death, and suffering. However, the common false solution is EARNING it through human law keeping, good deeds, or religious efforts. We can't add any works to Jesus though!

Colossians 2:8 says,

"See to it that no one takes you captive through hollow and deceptive philosophy, which depends on human tradition and the elemental spiritual forces of this world rather than on Christ."

Galatians 2:16 says,

"A person is not justified by the works of the law, but by faith in Jesus Christ. So we, too, have put our faith in Christ Jesus that we may be justified by faith in Christ and not by the works of the law, because by the works of the law no one will be justified."

FALSE SPIRITUALITY

This is any pursuit of mystical experience that is spiritually counterfeit and harmful. The first philosophy is Gnosticism. This aims to FIND salvation, pleasure, knowledge, or power through secret hidden (occult) means and mystical practices. They all attempt to connect to the spiritual realm in forbidden ways.

Examples include New Age, Shamanism, Spiritism, Tribal Nature religions, Scientology, Freemasonry, Kabbalah (Jewish mysticism), and Wicca. Most include divination or witchcraft rituals, using amulets for protection, seances, astrology, psychics, tarot cards, Ouija boards, seeking angels, channeling spirits, speaking with the dead, offering blood sacrifices. Deuteronomy. 18:9-13 God said,

> *"When you enter the land the Lord your God is giving you, do not learn to imitate the detestable ways of the nations there. Let no one be found among you who sacrifices their son or daughter in the fire, who practices divination or sorcery, interprets omens, engages in witchcraft, or casts spells, or who is a medium or spiritist or who consults the dead. Anyone who does these things is detestable to the Lord; because of these same detestable practices the Lord your God will drive out those nations before you. You must be blameless before the Lord your God."*

Doing such things was actually Satan's first deception. God forbade Adam and Eve from eating the forbidden fruit and warned that if they ate it, it would kill them. Satan called God a liar who wanted to selfishly keep Adam and Eve from becoming a god like Him. Satan promised them that they wouldn't die, and that eating it would give them wisdom, understanding, and they would be like God. Obviously, Satan lied (Gen. 3:1-7).

Leviticus 19:31 God said,

> *"Do not turn to mediums or seek out spiritists, for you will be defiled by them. I am the Lord your God."*

These activities connect not to God, but to demons, for their power. And it comes with strings attached and deceitful knowledge that leads to death.

The second philosophy is Enlightenment. This version is about trying to UNLOCK salvation from within by destroying the ego (self) and all human desires. Examples include Hinduism and Buddhism.

It's believed God isn't the personal creator of the universe and human suffering isn't caused by sin or evil. Rather God is the universe and everything in it (including humans) are a part of God. Since it's an illusion that we actually exist as individuals, it's our selfish pursuits and "attachment to desires" that cause suffering. But no, it is the selfish aims and sins that cause suffering!

The solution is not to believe that we are a part of God, and use mindless meditation, mantras, chants, and yoga to empty our minds and desires to become a hollow shell of our true selves. That's a way to empty your car and invite demons in! The solution is to do what Mark 12:30-31 says,

> "Love the Lord your God with all your heart and with all your soul and with all your mind and with all your strength.' [and] 'Love your neighbor as yourself.'"

CARNAL COMPROMISE

Usually accompanied by false beliefs, this is any sinful compromise caused by the pursuit of worldly pleasure. The philosophy is Hedonism. This about living like only pleasure matters by trying to INDULGE in carnal pleasures and pursue natural desires.

This is adopted by atheist and naturalistic worldviews but it's also a snare for Christians. Many people, even entire denominations, have derailed their faith with "inclusive / progressive" lies that Christians can have an active lifestyle as someone gay, bi, transgender, or questionable gender. They're allowing their sinful feelings to determine their identity instead of God's Word.

Others may have correct biblical Christian identity and beliefs but then accept the lie that since they're saved by grace and Jesus paid for their sins it's optional for them to live holy and righteous. No! Those engaging in sexual immorality, fornication, abortion, strip clubs, pornography, drunkenness, recreational drugs, blasphemy, theft, lying, crude behavior, vulgar language, gossip, or slander, are deceived and many not saved though they think they are. Galatians 5:19-21 says,

> *The acts of the flesh are obvious: sexual immorality, impurity and debauchery; idolatry and witchcraft; hatred, discord, jealousy, fits of rage, selfish ambition, dissensions, factions and envy; drunkenness, orgies, and the like. I warn you, as I did before, that those who live like this will not inherit the kingdom of God."*

1 John 3:2-6 says,

> *"When Christ appears, we shall be like him, for we shall see him as he is. All who have this hope in him purify themselves, just as he is pure. Everyone who sins breaks the law; in fact, sin is lawlessness. But you know that he appeared so that he might take away our sins. And in him is no sin. No one who lives in him keeps on sinning. No one who continues to sin has either seen him or known him."*

Romans 12:1 says,

> *"Offer your bodies as a living sacrifice, holy and pleasing to God."*

COUNTERFEIT JESUSES

This is any false version of Jesus that distorts someone's ability to know the true God or trust in the true gospel. The aim of Satan here is to Distort Biblical (Saving) Christianity. Unable to prevent people from hearing about Jesus and having access to the Bible, Satan invented false versions of Jesus and other ways to hide or distort essential biblical truths.

These false versions, that will not save, include Jesus as: the first created spirit being (Jehovah's Witnesses); a human prophet (Islam); an enlightened human teacher (Christian Science, Unity School of Christianity, Unitarian Universalist, New Age); a spirit child from sex between Father and Mother God who were both once human beings (Latter Day Saints / Mormons).

PRAYER

LORD God, remove in me every stronghold and foothold connected to a false religion, false spirituality, carnal compromise, or counterfeit Jesus. Sanctify every part of me. In Jesus' name. Amen.

JOURNAL

1. Which one of the four categories has had the largest mental or emotional stronghold in your life? Was there a specific belief you were raised into, or a sin you had fallen for because it appealed to you?

2. Renounce all of them, especially those you've been personally involved with. Do it out loud verbally and in written form in your journal. Renounce them as sinful lies you want nothing to do with. If you feel demonic resistance when doing so, fight hard to keep going until you feel them release. Ask God to deliver you from them, and command every demon to leave you in Jesus' name.

3. Declare verbally, and in your writing, positive statements that affirm the truth i.e. Jesus is God, homosexuality is sin, etc. You can do this for any false or sinful thing, it will help break ancestral curses you may be unaware of. But especially do this for any areas that you have been personally involved with. When you're all finished, ask God to fill every part of you, now vacated, with the presence of the Holy Spirit.

Day 11

Close these 8 Open Doors & keep Satan out

You must remain vigilant, because as 1 Peter 5:8-9 says,

> "Be alert and of sober mind. Your enemy the devil prowls around like a roaring lion looking for someone to devour."

Ephesians 6:16 says,

> "Take up the shield of faith, with which you can extinguish all the flaming arrows of the evil one."

These farther away attacks are going to be more subtle and less obvious. However, Ephesians 6:11-12 says,

> "Put on the full armor of God, so that you can take your stand against the devil's schemes. For our struggle is not against flesh and blood, but against the rulers, against the authorities, against the powers of this dark world and against the spiritual forces of evil in the heavenly realms."

Our struggle with demons is like a wrestling bout or a street fight. They attack in up-close, comprehensive, and sophisticated ways. Demons custom-design their attacks specifically to target your areas of greatest temptation, brokenness, weakness, or vulnerability.

They're experts at causing intense pain, fear, doubt, anxiety, temptation, and hindrance to your faith and walk with God. Examine yourself for possible vulnerabilities in these 8 open doors to close them and keep Satan out.

FALSE BELIEFS

You abandoned many core false beliefs when you became a Christian, but demons are trying to reestablish them by tempting you to return to them. They're also trying to fortify the false spiritual beliefs you still have in ignorance. So continue to learn and grow in the truth.

They may also target you with cognitive biases and logical fallacies. These are systematic errors in your disposition, mental processing, or reasoning that affect the decisions and judgments you make.

They're also targeting your limiting beliefs. These are often subconscious beliefs, stories, or excuses you tell yourself that limit you from reaching your full potential.

You must regularly reinforce and grow in your knowledge of, and commitment to, biblical beliefs. You must continually guard your mind from false thoughts entering in, and when questionable thoughts enter, always test and evaluate them before accepting them as true. Always seek to grow and renew your mind in truth.

FALSE REPENTANCE AND FAITH

When you repented and gave your life to Jesus it was the beginning of a new permanent way of life. Repentance of sin and confession of faith aren't just a one-time decision to start your journey as a Christian. It was the first day of thousands where you'll continue to repeat or renew that action.

You'll repent of any recent sin and renew your trust in the gospel for forgiveness. Every day you're to renew your decision to live righteous pleasing God and trusting in Jesus. Demons will try to get you to backslide, living in sin or doubting the gospel. Revelation 2:5 Jesus said,

> "Repent and do the things you did at first. If you do not repent, I will come to you and remove your lampstand from its place."

CARNAL DESIRE

Demons aren't only concerned with absolute evil behavior. They are stoking any sinful hedonistic desire still in your heart to pursue worldly pleasure. They know if you love something you're more likely to compromise in sin to have it. Root out not only the external sin but the internal.

Examine your heart. What do you live for? What do you desire? What motivates you? Don't just clean up the outside that others can see. Jesus called the pharisees who did this "whitewashed tombs." (Matt. 23:27). They looked nice on the outside but were dead on the inside. Don't just treat symptoms. Get to the root heart desire of your needs, goals, behaviors and habits.

HYPER-GRACE

This is the philosophy that God's grace is so ample it outweighs His virtue and justice. Those holding this reason that since Jesus paid for all sins—past, present, and future—righteous behavior is optional.

A companion to this way of thinking is called Free Grace Theology. I have long form videos on our YouTube channel which expose this in detail. Proponents of this harmful theology often accuse Christians like myself who impose the requirement that believers must have righteous moral behavior of being a "religious work." They accuse Christians that believe they must live morally as trying to do good works that are helping to save them, in addition to faith, and are now thus guilty of "works salvation." That we're trying to earn our salvation by being moral.

The truth is that God is gracious, and it's true that we're saved by grace alone though faith alone in Christ alone—but not by a faith that is alone. Biblical faith is inseparable from repentance and obedience. Any excuse for why you can be saved while continuing to live sinfully is a demonic lie that appeals to a sin nature that's supposed to be dead! Romans 6:1-2 says,

> *"Shall we go on sinning so that grace may increase? Certainly not! How can we who died to sin still live in it any longer?"*

Even if alongside otherwise correct Christian doctrines and religious practices these ungodly beliefs and desires nonetheless still deny Jesus as Lord.

Jude 1:4 says,

> *"They are ungodly people, who pervert the grace of our God into a license for immorality and deny Jesus Christ our only Sovereign and Lord."*

EMOTIONAL BROKENNESS

One of the most common open doors to demons is emotional wounds. This could be unhealed traumas, disassociated identities, unforgiveness, bitterness, anxiety, depression, hatred, guilt, shame, or mental health issues.

Demons are often exacerbating, if not outright causing the problem, and utilizing it as their stronghold into your life. Bring all these emotional skeletons out of the dark closet and expose them to the light of Christ. Examine your life and heart for any areas needing God's healing.

TOXIC RELATIONSHIPS

Demons strategically use people to steal, kill, and destroy. They'll influence others to be abusive and toxic to you. And then they'll come on the other side and influence you with the false belief that it's not only permissible but actually good for you to stay and endure it! I hear all the time from believers who are putting up with outright abuse and doing it in the name of Christian love, covenant, forgiveness, or in order to a witness to them! However, we have been commanded in the Bible:

1. Not to allow our love for anyone else to supersede our love for Jesus. He is to always come first (Matt. 10:37)

2. To put our eternal identity, calling and spiritual health first (Matt. 19:29)

3. To distance ourselves from fellowship with unrepentant sinful people who are harming us spiritually or otherwise (Matt. 18:17; 1 Cor. 5)

4. To not be unequally yoked with unbelievers (2 Cor. 6:14)

Yes, God sets up divine appointments and connections with other people to bless us. But I have news for you. Satan can do the same thing to harm us. Just because there's a supernatural or providential "coincidence" connecting you to someone, don't automatically assume that this is from God. Test it out and evaluate it based on the fruit.

Demons can also get to you by orchestrating "divine" connections with others with whom they already have a stronghold or an open door with. Since the relationship is assumed to be from God, people just jump all in to major decisions without caution, prayer, or wise counsel. Demons then exploit each person's sins or weaknesses that perfectly work against and harm one other. Examine your life for any relationships that are poisoning your walk with God.

TOXIC CONNECTIONS

Demons can gain access to you through a haunted residence or the possession of accursed objects. Remove anything accursed from your possession. Walk through your home, etc. and command any spirits not of God to leave in Jesus' name. Anoint the doors and windows of the home with oil, dedicating it to the Lord, and ask Him to bless it and fill it with His presence.

You could also have a toxic "spiritual" connections such as unbroken curses or ungodly soul ties with people or institutions. Break all of these by verbally renouncing all sin and ungodly attachment. Declare your faith in the truths of the gospel that break any connection you have to that brokenness.

TOXIC HABITS

Demons could be the instigator of a toxic desire, the toxic solution to an otherwise godly desire, or just be a cheerleader on the side reminding and encouraging your continuance in the toxic portions of your habit.

Every habit you have is meeting a need or desire. Detect any ungodly desires and crucify them. Detect godly desires being met in an ungodly, unhealthy way and replace it with a godly, healthy alternative.

PRAYER

LORD God, deliver me from all demonic influence. Sanctify every part of me. Close every open door, renew my mind, heal my heart, restore my soul and order all my steps. In Jesus' name. Amen.

JOURNAL

1. Which of the eight categories has had the largest mental or emotional stronghold in your life? Was there a specific belief you were raised into, or a sin you had fallen for because it appealed to you?

2. Renounce all of them, especially those you've been personally involved with. Do it out loud verbally and in written form in your journal, i.e. "I repent of…" Renounce them as sinful lies you want nothing to do with. If you feel demonic resistance

when doing so, fight hard to keep going until you feel them release. Ask God to deliver you from them, and command every demon to leave you now and never return, in Jesus' name.

3. Break any curses by renouncing and declaring your intention, i.e. "I repent of…" and "I break any connection to," etc. This can be done for any false, sinful, or toxic thing. Ask God to give you knowledge about what you should renounce or break. When you're all finished, ask God to fill every part of you, now vacated, with the presence of the Holy Spirit.

Day 12

8 Keys to a Mindset for Emotional Health and Success

Your life as a Christian should be enjoyable, not miserable and stressful. It won't always be easy or comfortable. God will definitely take you through difficulties that will challenge, refine, and develop you.

But your "inner life," your thoughts and beliefs, and how they affect your emotions, these can be managed to have peace, joy, and fulfillment within, regardless of your external situations. This lesson, you'll learn 8 keys to having a mindset for emotional health and success.

CRUCIFY OLD PATTERNS OF THINKING

To establish a new mindset you need to recognize and crucify your old patterns of thinking that harm and limit you. Often our old nature is much more familiar, real, or strong to us, than our faith in our new nature is. But you've been born again. You can change who you are in every other way because God now lives in you!

The old you is dead so don't allow old things to continue. Every sinful thought, belief, desire, or behavior causes bondage and death. Stop repeating things like, "I've always been this way" or any other excuse that keeps you the same. Sin is not a disease that needs to be managed. It's a cancer that needs to be removed! The first key is to crucify old patterns of thinking using a process that I call **TB-Fab:**

Change who you Become, by changing how you Act, by changing how you Feel, by changing what you Believe, by learning how to manage your Thoughts. It begins in the reverse order like this:

THINK > BELIEVE > FEEL > ACT > BE

Apply this process to the next 7 keys below. Ephesians 4:22-24 says,

> *"Put off your old self, which is being corrupted by its deceitful desires; to be made new in the attitude of your minds; and to put on the new self, created to be like God in true righteousness and holiness."*

EMBRACE YOUR RIGHTEOUSNESS IN CHRIST

Forget your past sins, faults, failures, and mistakes, and think about your newfound righteousness. Stop focusing on things you've already given to Jesus. Don't let yourself or Satan keep bringing up your past sins, faults, or failures so that you keep thinking and feeling guilty about them.

Often people do this and then they beat themselves up afterwards. Almost like feeling bad about it, or trying harder, or any other reactive way to respond is a type of punishment for what you did. It's almost like you're trying to do penance to pay the penalty for it yourself.

But if you do this, then you're not trusting in the gospel! Jesus already paid for it, and you've already received forgiveness and His imputed righteousness, so leave everything from the past in the past where it belongs.

EMBRACE YOUR NEW IDENTITY IN CHRIST

We all have things about ourselves we don't like. Things about the past we wish hadn't happened, or things about our present situation we wish were different. Don't let this fuel insecurities, comparison, envy, covetousness, hatred, blame or bitterness. Whatever you hate about who you were, died, so let go of it.

Focus not on others, but yourself, on what God's doing in and through you. He's not comparing you to others, He's comparing you to the old you! Focus on being less like the old you, the sinner, and more like the new you, in Christ. Focus on eternal things, being productive and fruitful, and fulfilling your calling. That's where your purpose and fulfillment will be found.

What's your highest identity? It should be a child of God and disciple of Jesus. Focus on these thoughts. 1 John 3:2 says,

> "Now we are children of God... when Christ appears, we shall be like him..."

HAVE ASSURANCE OF YOUR ELECTION

The Bible teaches that all of the elect will be saved. However, there are different views as to how a person becomes one of the elect.

In Reformed or Calvinistic soteriology (which just means the study of how salvation works), "the elect" are the people God chose to save even before they were born. It's God who 100% chooses who they are, enables only them to believe in Jesus, and saves only them. So basically God chooses them, rather than the other way around.

Satan exploits the weakness of this belief system by giving people intrusive thoughts to give up all faith and hope because no matter what they think, believe, or do, they're not elected. He bombards them with thoughts that Jesus didn't die for them, and their sins have not been forgiven. So, despite them believing the gospel, living right, and walking with the Lord, they're going to Hell anyways. Reject that demonic lie! John 3:16 says,

> "Whoever believes in him shall not perish but have eternal life."

Are you a whoever? Then Jesus died to save you! I believe in and recommend that everyone consider what is called the corporate view of election:

The elect are simply the total group of all being saved. People become a member of the elect when they freely choose to trust in Jesus. So you're not elected to believe; you believe and become one of the elect.

HAVE ASSURANCE OF YOUR SALVATION

The alternative soteriological views are Arminianism and Provisionism. Both of these views believe that we freely choose to repent and believe the gospel, so we could equally freely choose not to. Similar to the way Satan exploits the weaknesses of Calvinism to torment people to believe they're not saved, he also exploits the weaknesses of these systems too.

Since many with these views believe that salvation could be lost after once being saved, Satan sends intrusive thoughts that a person has already lost it and there's nothing they can do now to have it back. Or he sends tormenting thoughts that it could be lost at any point so people live depressed and legalistic, crippled by fear and anxiety.

The truth is salvation can be unreceived, or intentionally forsaken, but not accidentally lost. If you want to be saved and are walking right, then you are! And if you sin at some point in the future, Jesus is interceding for you on your behalf (1 John 2:1-2). You're not immediately cut off just because you sinned. Just repent and trust the gospel all over again. Hebrews 10:35 says,

> "Do not throw away your confidence; it will be richly rewarded."

HAVE ASSURANCE REGARDING "THE UNPARDONABLE SIN"

Like the previous two items, Satan also exploits how people misunderstand what the Unpardonable Sin, or "The Blasphemy of the Holy Spirit" is (Matt. 12:22-32; Mark 3:22-29). Jesus did that it is the only unforgivable sin, an eternal sin, and there is no way to be forgiven for it.

Satan may attack you by sending you thoughts that you've already committed this sin in the past, either by blaspheming God directly, or by ever questioning if some supernatural manifestation was truly the Holy Spirit responsible. But this is a demonic lie and twisting of what Jesus meant.

This is not something you could've done in the past. It's only something you can do now in the present. To commit this sin means to deny the testimony of the Holy Spirit by unambiguously, intentionally, and permanently rejecting Jesus as your Lord and Savior until death.

This isn't something any repentant, believing, obedient follower of Jesus should worry about. It's something unbelievers should worry about.

EMBRACE GOSPEL TRUTH REGARDING FUTURE SIN

Sin creates barriers of separation between us and God but it doesn't immediately cut us off. In Christ by faith, we're justified and adopted into God's family. Don't believe that if you commit a sin you're instantly unsaved again or God is mad and doesn't want you anywhere near Him.

You didn't stop being His child. Don't run away from God, or from the church, to try and clean yourself up before returning. Rather, run to Him and the church in repentance, trusting Jesus has already paid for it!

Sin isn't only outward actions, it's also our flesh nature. In other words, sin isn't only a behavior you can do. Sinful is a way of being. Sinful desires of your heart are still sin even if you don't act on them. The natural predisposition of our flesh is inherently sinful so sin will feel natural, normal, and right. This is why we must crucify it and choose to be led by the Spirit daily.

God gave us the Holy Spirit as a seal and deposit until the "perfect" comes later. God chose to allow us to wrestle with sin this way to keep choosing Him over and over. He is glorified in your struggle with sin! So it's OK to be tempted and it's forgivable if you stumble. He is using sin to make you more like Jesus, to keep renewing your faith in the gospel, and deepen your relationship with Him in order to overcome it. He doesn't expect you to be perfect; He expects you to keep trusting and depending on the One who is. 1 John 1:9, 2:2 says,

"If we confess our sins, he is faithful... and will forgive us... I write this... so that you will not sin. But if anybody does sin, we have an advocate...

Jesus Christ, the Righteous One."

COMMIT TO RENEWING YOUR MIND

Study and meditate on God's Word and truths therein and let God's thoughts and beliefs become yours. Romans 12:1-2 says,

> *"Offer your bodies as living sacrifices... be transformed by the renewing of your mind."*

And Philippians 4:8 says,

> *"Whatever is true... noble... right... pure... lovely... admirable—if anything is excellent or praiseworthy—think about such things."*

PRAYER

LORD God, help me manage my thoughts, put off my old self, and embrace the salvation Jesus purchased for me, and the righteousness, identity, and closeness it provides. In Jesus' name. Amen.

JOURNAL

1. Which of the eight keys best addresses an issue in your life? How will applying it help your faith and relationship with God?

2. Change is not easy and it takes time. My TB-Fab system has lead to great breakthrough for many people. Ask God what thoughts, beliefs, and behaviors you need to apply it towards.

3. Were you aware how many ways Satan harms people emotionally that could be fought by trusting the gospel? Ask the Lord to lay on your heart someone who needs assurance. Pray for them, then reach out to them today to talk with them about it.

Day 13

The 4 Habits of the emotionally resilient Christian

Resilience is the capacity to withstand, adapt, or recover quickly from difficult or challenging life experiences. Christians can improve their emotional resilience by disciplining themselves to give more of their focus to three essential truths of our faith:

Your salvation and eternal life has already been purchased and guaranteed on the basis of your faith in the finished work of Jesus alone.

God, your Heavenly Father, adopted you as His child and His Spirit supernaturally lives inside of you leading, sanctifying, and empowering you through your journey.

Jesus has already achieved the victory, you're guaranteed to win the final war, and He's with you empowering you to win every battle.

These core truths form the foundation for this lesson: The 4 habits of the emotionally resilient Christian.

HABIT #1: BE A PERSON OF ACTION NOT REACTION

John 7:38-39 Jesus said,

> "Whoever believes in me... rivers of living water will flow from within them." By this he meant the Spirit."

Supernatural life flows in your veins. God calls you to be a good tree that stewards the opportunities He's put before you. Spot and take advantage of them. Take initiative and do things without being told to. Find out what you need to know and where you need to grow. Remove bad fruit from your life and grow good fruit. Recall what we discussed yesterday, a process I call **TB-Fab:**

You can determine the kind of tree that you'll Become, by changing how you Act, by changing how you Feel, by changing what you Believe, by learning how to manage the Thoughts you allow yourself to think about.

THINK > BELIEVE > FEEL > ACT > BE

This lesson, we're focusing on the middle: how you feel. The emotions you consistently feel tell a lot about the actions you're likely to take. They also tell a lot about what you're letting yourself think about and believe in. A tree needs to be planted, take root, and then get watered to grow.

Likewise, how you feel day-to-day is directly related to what you think about, believe in, and water (or feed) regularly. Good thoughts lead to good emotions and good fruit. Bad thoughts lead to bad emotions and bad fruit.

If your emotional fruit is bad, trace it back to its origin and correct it. If you don't, you'll make the mistake of trying to treat your bad emotion or action symptoms, rather than their cause, the thoughts or beliefs.

You can change how you feel immediately. Examine every thought and determine whether to focus on it or discard it. Don't believe or feed into the lies of the enemy or the concerns of the world. Believe the truth of God's Word and feed into it. Do this consistently and you'll feel the grace and joy of God overflowing in your inner spirit like rivers of living water, regardless of what life's throwing at you.

Next, you'll learn three habits to think, believe, and feed into regularly to build greater emotional resilience and be more empowered to take greater action and make a difference.

HABIT #2: CARRY AN ATTITUDE OF GRATITUDE

Psychiatrist and Holocaust survivor Victor Frankl said,

> "Everything can be taken from a man but one thing: the last of human freedoms- to choose one's attitude in any given set of circumstances, to choose one's own way." [2]

Even in the worst situations imaginable, we still always have the liberty to choose how we respond. We either follow our flesh and react in a sinful way, or consciously use the moment as an opportunity to glorify God.

Even nonbelievers see the benefits of just trying to be a generally grateful person. But the truth is that for us who believe the Bible, gratitude is not just some technique to improve how we feel. We truly do, literally, have so much to be grateful for! And that is still true even if this life has nothing to offer us but suffering and martyrdom. Because this life is not the end for those who believe!

Colossians 2:7 Paul says to live overflowing with thankfulness the same as when you first believed the gospel. Gratitude to God should be the foundation under everything else we think and feel. Learning to trust God through challenges that test your resolve, while leaning in to Him to maintain your gratitude, will develop your spiritual maturity. Gratitude lays the foundation for our thoughts to always be stable, fixed on what's good, so that we're never double-minded (James 1:5-8). Colossians 3:15-17 says,

> "Let the peace of Christ rule in your hearts... And be thankful. Let the message of Christ dwell among you richly... singing to God with gratitude in your hearts. And whatever you do, whether in word or deed, do it all in the name of the Lord Jesus, giving thanks to God the Father through him."

HABIT #3: CARRY A CONQUEROR MENTALITY

Think, believe, and feel like a victor—rather than a victim. Some people embrace their victim identity, even meeting their human need for significance and comfort from it. Still others embrace their victimhood because they get sympathy, support, and human connection from others through it. But despite the fact that a victim mentality has some utility, it isn't good.

If you have been victimized, and just about everyone has to one extent or another, then perhaps your victim mentality is justifiable and warranted. You were the victim of someone or something, so you have a right to claim your victimhood. But you need to realize that there's no good fruit to be gained by believing and feeling that way long-term. Get the therapy and healing you need and then put that victimization behind you.

Romans 8:37-39 says,

> *"We are more than conquerors through him who loved us. For I am convinced that neither death nor life... angels nor demons... present nor the future, nor any powers... height nor depth, nor anything else in all creation, will be able to separate us from the love of God that is in Christ Jesus our Lord."*

Stop identifying as the victim of sin, Satan, or circumstances. See yourself as the conqueror of sin, Satan, and circumstances. The victim mentality is a thought you can believe and feed, or disbelieve and discard. If you feed the identity and thought that "I'm a victim," I guarantee you it will bear fruit of hopelessness, depression, anxiety, fear, pessimism, blaming, resentment, anger, unaccountability, apathy, etc.

Rather, choose to bear the fruit of a conqueror: hope, peace, joy, confidence, optimism, accountability, forgiveness, boldness, and courage. Those who trust in the Lord will be victorious. Take hold of His victory and set your focus on it. You'll get freedom in the soul and joy in the Spirit, regardless of your past circumstances, or future ones.

DAY 13 - THE 4 HABITS OF THE EMOTIONALLY RESILIENT CHRISTIAN

HABIT #4: CARRY OPTIMISTIC GLASSES

John 16:33 Jesus said,

> "In me you may have peace. In this world you will have trouble. But take heart! I have overcome the world."

Optimism is the disposition or tendency to look on the more favorable side of events or conditions and expect the most favorable outcome. Pessimism is the opposite and it is inconsistent with Christianity.

We know that God is sovereign (in control of the big picture), that all things work together for our good long term (Rom. 8:28), that the best is yet to come, and even if bad things happen they are an opportunity to glorify God while deepening our growth and relationship with Him. Optimism is the outlook that will move resilience and faith into action.

1 Peter 1:13 says,

> "Therefore, preparing your minds for action, and being sober-minded, set your hope fully on the grace that will be brought to you at the revelation of Jesus Christ." (ESV)

PRAYER

Heavenly Father, help me be a person of action, emotionally resilient, with an attitude of gratitude and a conqueror mentality, seeing trials optimistically as opportunities. In Jesus' name. Amen.

JOURNAL

1. Which of the four habits is speaking most to you today? Talk with God about it. Confess not doing enough of it. Ask Him for insights to better embrace it has a regular habit going forward.

2. Meditate on these habits. How would your thought life and emotional life improve if these were your "normal/regular" way of thinking? Spend some time in prayer asking the Father to give you more of the fullness of this in your life beginning with today.

3. Which of the habits mentioned are you already embracing often and very confident in? Ask God to highlight someone in your mind that struggles in that area that He would like you to reach out to today about it.

Day 14

8 Lifestyle Behaviors of the emotionally resilient Christian

Emotional resilience is the capacity to withstand, adapt, or recover emotionally quickly through challenging life situations. This lesson surveys 8 lifestyle behaviors that build your emotional resilience and help ensure that your Christian journey is more fruitful and enjoyable.

A LIFESTYLE OF PRAYER AND INTIMACY WITH GOD

Prayer, via intimacy with God, is the hallmark behavior of the Christian life. Prayer is simply communication with God. It's you talking with God and God talking with you.

Prayer is the glue between Bible Study (God speaking to you through His Word) and Worship (you seeking God's presence and singing to Him). It's where knowledge and experience meet, and relationship intimacy is deepened.

Your prayers will more often be verbal words spoken to God. It's also good to pray in written form in a journal. You can also pray in your heavenly language (praying or signing in tongues), or any other form of praying in the Spirit.

Prayers are not better or more effective just because they're longer, Jesus specifically told us this (Matt. 6:7). Nor are they better when they're louder. Some charismatics act like God would prefer us to shout it at Him! Nor does God care if they are impressively spoken. The Lord careth-not if you know thy King James-speak and do-so welleth. ;-) And while I'm at it, God is also OK with you taking pauses to hear from the Holy Spirit or to think about what you want to say. You don't have to say Lord, Father, God, or other iterations of His name eight million times and fill in all the silence with words constantly. God isn't going to hang up the phone just because you paused to take a breath between sentences.

Talk to God as though you know Him and actually have a relationship with Him. And like conversation in any other relationship, what matters most is love, sincerity, and the pursuit of closeness during your interaction.

For 4 types of prayer remember the acronym ACTS: Adoration, Confession, Thanksgiving, and Supplication. Things that will hinder your prayers include: unforgiveness, insincerity, doubt, sinfulness, and worldly motives. Prayer should not be your last resort. It should be your first response. 1 John 3:21-22 says,

> "Dear friends, if our hearts do not condemn us, we have confidence before God and receive from him anything we ask, because we keep his commands and do what pleases him."

A LIFESTYLE OF WORSHIP

Worship is an ongoing attitude and posture to always have. Worshipping with music is good. Ephesians 5:19-20 says,

> "Sing and make music from your heart to the Lord, always giving thanks to God the Father for everything, in the name of our Lord Jesus Christ."

However, worship of God is not always music and singing, even though music and singing to God is always worship. God rebuked people for worshipping idols even when they weren't doing musical performances. Those people had invested into those idols their faith, their trust, their devotion, and their sacrificial offerings. Our worship to God should also include all these things.

Your entire existence should be full of ways you're worshipping God by who you are and how you live for His glory. The Father is seeking those who love Him with all their heart, mind, soul, and strength, and worship Him in spirit and truth (Mark 12:30; John 4:23-24). Your REAL worship is what you do with the other 167 hours of the week outside of the church walls! Colossians 3:17 says,

> "Whatever you do, whether in word or deed, do it all in the name of the Lord Jesus, giving thanks to God the Father through him."

A LIFESTYLE OF REPENTANCE AND CONFESSION

To repent means to change your direction away from going towards sin and going in the opposite direction towards God. Expect and encourage some beliefs and desires to evolve during your journey. If they aren't, you're not spiritually maturing. Have an I'm-always-improving mindset.

Romans 10:10 says,

> "For with the heart one believes... and with the mouth one confesses." (ESV)

1 John 1:9 says,

> "If we confess our sins, he... will forgive... and purify us from all unrighteousness."

James 5:16 says,

> "Therefore confess your sins to each other and pray for each other so that you may be healed. The prayer of a righteous person is powerful and effective."

A LIFESTYLE OF BIBLICAL FAITH (NOT WORD OF FAITH)

Continue to grow in faith but be sure that you're not being influenced by Word Faith theology. Word Faith theology comes out of the New Thought movement which is New Age and not biblical or Christian at all. Word of Faith theology is a perversion of what true biblical faith is, is an overemphasis on health and wealth, and it is a poison in the church.

Faith is not a spiritual force or law of the universe to tap into to get whatever our carnal heart wants. Faith is trust in a personal God who is trustworthy.

Spiritual healing was purchased on the cross and it is available now. And yes, God does still heal physically but He doesn't always as long as we have enough faith. The "Prosperity Gospel" opposes Jesus' command to be cross-bearing disciples. The kind of faith God wants us to have is the kind of faith that trusts Him enough to obey and follow His will even when it's not going to lead to worldly comforts and pleasure in this life. There will be suffering in this life. Suffering isn't good, but God does always use it for good. 1 Timothy 6:6-11 says,

> "Godliness with contentment is great gain. Those who want to be rich... fall into temptation and become ensnared by many foolish and harmful desires that plunge them into ruin and destruction... flee from these things and pursue righteousness, godliness, faith, love, perseverance."

A LIFESTYLE OF RIGHTEOUS SPIRITUAL WARFARE

We're at war. You've been given the authority and name of Christ to use against Satan. But if you believe Satan's lie that most problems are caused by sin, then they'll exploit your ignorance, faithlessness, fear, and desire for comfort.

You already have what you need for victory over the forces of darkness but you must faithfully and deliberately exercise it over them. All believers can command demons to leave dwellings and even to come out of people, not just the ordained or specially gifted. If you're born again you have authority of Christ against them, and the power given by the Holy Spirit inside of you.

Whenever and however you need to fight Satan, whether just in intercessory prayer or outright exorcism of people, always have righteous decorum and do it a morally righteous way. The same way that Jesus did. We are spiritual warriors but we're also God's children. We fight motivated by love, truth, and justice.

A LIFESTYLE OF BIBLICAL DECLARATIONS

Fight Satan and shift the spiritual atmosphere with warfare prayers, which are really just declarations. A declaration is a verbal profession, but it has power against the supernatural forces of evil when:

1. Declaring a biblical truth
2. Inspired by the Holy Spirit living within a person
3. Aligned with one's personal faith in the declaration
4. Driven by godly motives that glorify God

When Satan lies, dismiss his accusations, thoughts, and emotions, confidently responding with truth from God's Word. Ephesians 6:17 says,

> "Take... the sword of the Spirit, which is the word of God."

Satan may still cause chaos in the world on the outside, but inside your soul should be the presence and joy of the Lord!

A LIFESTYLE OF OVERCOMING

You've been given supernatural power to overcome. 1 John 5:4 says,

> "For everyone who has been born of God overcomes the world. And this is the victory that has overcome the world—our faith." (ESV)

When trouble comes, let it find your unshakable faith! Don't fear or be overwhelmed. You can achieve victory in every battle. Ephesians 3:20 says,

> "Now to Him who is able to do immeasurably more than all we ask or imagine, according to His power that is at work within us."

You can crucify your old patterns of thinking, control your thoughts, and focus more on your new identity and purpose in Christ, as well as on your eternal destination and less on this world. You can renew your mind in God's Word daily and walk in supernatural power and hopeful confidence of victory.

A LIFESTYLE OF ENDURANCE

Sometimes victory will be glorifying God through the way we endure our trial, rather than actually being delivered from it. This is a tough truth but it comes with it a blessing in disguise. Everyone in Christ has been given supernatural power by the Spirit to endure. James 5:10-11 says,

> "As an example of patience in the face of suffering, take the prophets... we count as blessed those who have persevered."

Colossians 1:10-11 says,

> "Live a life worthy of the Lord... bearing fruit in every good work... being strengthened with all power according to his glorious might so that you may have great endurance and patience."

From right thoughts and emotions flow right words and behavior. Philippians 4:12-13 says,

DAY 14 - 8 LIFESTYLE BEHAVIORS OF THE EMOTIONALLY RESILIENT CHRISTIAN

"I have learned the secret of being content in any and every situation, whether well fed or hungry, whether living in plenty or in want. I can do all this through him who gives me strength."

PRAYER

Heavenly Father, help me to have a lifestyle of prayer, intimacy, worship, repentance, faith, truth, confession, righteous decorum, and victory or endurance in every trial. In Jesus' name. Amen.

JOURNAL

1. Which of the eight lifestyle behaviors have you been most neglecting? How will applying this new understanding help your faith and relationship with God? Talk with Him about it.

2. Having regular emotional resilience, much less walking in a supernaturally high degree of resilience takes time. Ask God which of these eight behaviors you should focus on for the rest of today.

3. Plan out a few ways to embrace this behavior throughout the rest of the day. Pray and ask God to interrupt you later and remind you throughout the day to approach your day with this in mind.

Day 15

The Fruitfulness of your Life shows your Direction

The road to Hell is paved with good intentions. History records many people who desired a good outcome but pursued it in ways that caused a lot of evil. They believed they were working toward Heaven on earth, but if they'd known what God actually wanted, and looked at the fruitfulness of the road they were on, they would've noticed all the signs pointing to Hell.

There's harm in claiming to go in the direction towards eternal life with God, without paying careful attention to the journey. It's better to take a single step in the right direction than to figuratively move mountains in the wrong direction. If you're going in the right direction, towards eternal life with God, it will be fruitful. Picture lots of healthy fruit trees on both sides of the road in that direction.

Good fruit is anything that brings glory to God. So, as you're making decisions, go in the direction of fruitfulness, seeking good fruit as a goal, confirming that you're seeing good fruit as a result. Pursue a life of planting, watering, growing, cultivating, and harvesting good fruit.

Eternal life with Jesus is your destination, but fruit is your compass. It will tell you which way is true north.

DAY 15 - THE FRUITFULNESS OF YOUR LIFE SHOWS YOUR DIRECTION

This lesson covers:

1. Good fruit must be an expression of God
2. Good fruit only comes from good trees
3. Good fruit must do the Father's will

GOOD FRUIT MUST BE AN EXPRESSION OF GOD

Fruit is only good when it's an accurate expression of God's character and will. God decides what's good and what isn't. History is filled with awful people who had their own definition of good and evil. In fact, most of the greatest evils were committed by those thinking they're doing what is good from their perspective.

Everything from Adam and Eve eating the forbidden fruit, to Hitler's effort to establish a socialist utopia. We can't forget these lessons and risk making the same mistakes, deciding for ourselves what is good or bad.

We also can't chase even something God calls good and just focus on that. For example, the Bible says God is love and love is good. Does this mean that anything called an act of love is good? What if an action being called a loving action is called sinful by God? The Bible says that polygamous, homosexual, bestial, and incestuous relationships are bad. It says that all sexual activity outside of a one-man, one-woman marriage covenant is bad.

But what if they claim to love each other? If love is good, does that make these acts good? Do we go in the direction of "all that is love is good" or in the direction of "all God says is good is good?" Who decides?

What's our highest principle? What determines everything else? The reality is that love, honor, justice, grace, mercy, trust, integrity, joy, peace—these are only good because they're attributes of God. Anytime we put even good things above God and His will, it's idolatry. The sun is good, we need sun rays to have life, but if we worship the sun then it's an idol. So even good things, if we serve and chase them as our primary fruit, that will also lead us astray into sin.

God Himself is the highest value, highest good, and only judge. If anything opposes His will, it's evil. As you head towards good fruit, you'll be tempted create your own standards. It's crucial that you not chase the fruits themselves, but God. Don't chase the fruit—chase after the God of the fruit!

GOOD FRUIT ONLY COMES FROM GOOD TREES

How do you make sure you're chasing God Himself and not outward fruits? Focus on yourself first, on being a good tree. Matthew 7:17-19 Jesus said,

> *"Every good tree bears good fruit, but a bad tree bears bad fruit. A good tree cannot bear bad fruit, and a bad tree cannot bear good fruit. Every tree that does not bear good fruit is cut down and thrown into the fire."*

If you're a good tree you'll naturally, consistently bear good fruit. It's not optional. If you aim toward fruit you'll end up with legalism, chasing outward works in your own strength and get burned out. Pursing works this way is self-aggrandizing, not God-glorifying. Pursuing works this way causes fear, anxiety, doubts of salvation and relationship with God, because everything is based on the outward results. If outward works seem like they're not working, their marriage fails, or bad things happen, their faith can be shipwrecked.

Instead, if we aim towards being a good tree, good outward works will inevitably follow because they're just the byproduct of a good nature and character. They'll come as a result of God working in and through you, and be inspired, led, and empowered by Him. They'll come naturally and be in line with His will for your life. You'll have your relationship with God and identity grounded first, and thus do great things without worrying about the results. Matthew 18:3-4 Jesus said,

> *"Unless you change and become like little children, you will never enter the kingdom of heaven... whoever takes the lowly position of this child is the greatest in the kingdom of heaven."*

God's kingdom is different from those of the world. He desires in us humbleness, innocence, a sense of awe in who He is, and a childlike faith and trust in Him. If we're only after fruit, law keeping or good deeds, we'll totally miss this. We'll become legalists, religious lawyers, with strict adherence to God's laws, even otherwise good ones, yet still totally miss the point. We'll trust in our own efforts and lose all sense of awe in God, sense of mystery, all sense of trusting in Him.

The mystery of the Holy Trinity, the Incarnation, and every part of the Gospel and life with Jesus teach us not to be like this, but many still fall prey to it. The Kingdom of God is full of people like humble children with childlike faith trusting in God, not those boasting or trusting in their own works. This is the kind of tree to be and the type of fruitfulness to bear.

GOOD FRUIT MUST DO THE FATHER'S WILL

Our fruitfulness is built on the foundation of, trust in and obedience to, God's will. God considers fruitful behavior that which is in line with His will—regardless of what it looks like outwardly.

Is it more fruitful to help a thousand people or one person God told you to help? The one! It's better to obey God's will, trusting that He knows better than you, and He is the judge. The good fruit here is trust, surrender, and obedience even when it doesn't seem best in our opinion.

The fruit the Father seeks is HIS will to be done, on earth, as it is in Heaven. It's better to be obedient to God, in what seems like a small work to you, than to be disobedient to God to do what seems like a big work to you. Our goal is to please God, not chase the fruit. 1 Samuel 15:22 says,

> *"Does the LORD delight in burnt offerings and sacrifices as much as in obeying the LORD? To obey is better than sacrifice, and to heed is better than the fat of rams. For rebellion is like the sin of divination, and arrogance like the evil of idolatry."*

Also see Mark 3:35; Jeremiah 42:6; James 4:13-15; and 1 Peter 3:17.

PRAYER

Heavenly Father, make me a good tree reflecting Your character, obediently doing Your will. Help me be humble with childlike trust in You, bearing much fruit for Your glory. In Jesus' name. Amen.

JOURNAL

1. What is something that you have made a "highest good," even over God? Ask God to reveal it to you, help you understand how you did that, and why it was wrong to do.

2. What are some ways you've prioritized outward fruitfulness of society change and things others should do differently, above the inward change of moral righteousness in yourself? Talk to God about this and ask Him to give you understanding as to why you were doing that.

3. Ask God what His will is for you to do today. Be obedient and do it.

Day 16

God Demands Moral Righteousness and Justice

What kind of world does God want? One overflowing with moral righteousness and justice. He not only wants it, He demands it! Previously, we discussed how everyone going toward the destination of eternal life with God, will on their journey, bear lots of good fruit.

This lesson, we will examine different kinds of fruitfulness and how you should be prioritizing them.

IT'S FRUITFUL TO OBEY GOD'S LAW

The Torah, also called the Pentateuch, are the first five books of the Hebrew Scriptures and Christian Bibles. In these pages are lots of history but also God's laws, commands, and decrees. We informally summarize this and call it "God's Law." For example, Psalm 1:1-3 says,

> *"Blessed is the one who does not walk in step with the wicked... but whose delight is in the law of the LORD... who meditates on his law day and night. That person is like a tree planted by streams of water, which yields its fruit... whatever they do prospers."*

God commanded fruitful living and warned of the consequences of disobeying. God's Law reveals that God cares both about personal ethical morality for individuals, as well as justice within the governing of society. The Law includes positive commands, or things for them to do, and negative commands, or things for them not to do.

Of the 613 total individual laws, many were Ceremonial and related to the priesthood system, these Jesus completely fulfilled on our behalf.

Many were Civil, these instructed how to govern Israel to be holy and distinct from other nations. As Christians, we're not under these laws but we can learn a lot of wisdom about how to live from them.

Lastly, there were the Moral laws which teach us how to relate to God and one another. The New Testament repeatedly commands to observe and obey every moral law. Jesus did also fulfill the moral law for us to make us perfect under it. However, He also commanded us to live according to an even higher moral standard than the law, actually raising the bar for us (Matt. 5:17-48).

The Law was given as a tutor to help us know God and walk in His ways (Gal. 3:24). We're no longer under the Law but Grace (Rom. 6:14-15), so apply God's Law to your life taking into account the gospel.

HOW TO PRIORITIZE YOUR EFFORT FOR A FRUITFUL LIFE

Luke 3:8-9 John the Baptist says,

> *"Produce fruit in keeping with repentance... The ax is already at the root of the trees, and every tree that does not produce good fruit will be cut down and thrown into the fire."*

Before worrying about producing good fruit start by stopping producing bad fruit! A fruitful life begins with obedience to God's Moral Law and repentance. Use an inside-out approach. Begin with Inward Fruit First starting within your own heart and life. Galatians 5:22 says,

> *"The fruit of the Spirit is love, joy, peace, forbearance, kindness, good-*

ness, faithfulness, gentleness and self-control. Against such things there is no law."

Inner transformation comes before outer transformation. Church leaders were always chosen by godliness—not experience, gifting, status, skill or talent. They prioritized being full of the Spirit and wisdom (Acts 6:3), being above reproach, temperate, self-controlled, respectable, hospitable, dignified, sexual fidelity, and managing their household well (1 Tim. 3:2-4).

Next, Outward Fruit Flows from the inward fruit of our heart outwards to our attitudes, actions, behaviors and habits. This is why we mustn't focus on merely changing our external habits or behavior. Because it's only treating the symptom it's not a long term solution, nor does it make us like Jesus, because it doesn't allow the Holy Spirit to sanctify our soul.

CHANGE SPECTRUM

I developed a Spectrum for Change with 5 progressive levels. They should be prioritized in this order:

1. *Level 1* is Individual Internal Change through inward repentance, personal private victory over sin, character growth and development.

2. *Level 2* is Individual External Change, all behavior that affects others. This should also take the inside-out approach. First improve yourself, then your marriage, then as parent, group or church member, coworker, neighbor.

3. *Level 3* is creating Community Impact working with others through organized local action programs.

4. *Level 4* is Systemic Change through communities working together to promote biblical justice.

5. *Level 5* is Societal Change by communities and systems working together towards social or global reform.

PARTICIPATING IN FRUITFUL BIBLICAL AND SOCIAL JUSTICE

As you progress outwards towards bearing external fruit in society pursue justice. Biblical Justice is based on the just character of God, and His will for humanity, because each person is a coequal bearer of His image. Since all humans are created equal, justice applies to everyone equally under God's Law. This is the foundation for justice: equality under God. There's only two classes: God's, and the class of everyone else!

The word justice has been hijacked and changed to mean equity instead of equality. Equity means pursuing avenues of equal fairness, so it's not more difficult for some to succeed in life than others, or so that there's an equal distribution of prosperity in life. Equity is about correcting imbalances so there's an equal outcome for everyone.

Biblical justice is about equality, not equity. It's not about ensuring equal outcomes but equal opportunity. An unjust system is one that's been perverted so that some benefit at the expense of others. Biblical justice is about equality of dignity as a person, equality of the same human rights, equality of being under the same laws, so all have the same punishment for disobedience to the law, and same protection under the law. Biblical justice is always connected to righteous behavior. Deuteronomy 16:19-20 God says,

> *"Do not pervert justice or show partiality. Do not accept a bribe, for a bribe blinds the eyes of the wise and twists the words of the innocent. Follow justice and justice alone, so that you may live..."*

In Psalm 89:14 the psalmist said of God,

> *"Righteousness and justice are the foundation of your throne."*

Modern Social Justice has both ungodly and godly elements. Ungodly is when equity rather than equality is the outcome, especially when it's forced upon people in a biblically unjust way to supposedly benefit a so-called oppressed group. Thus, some are committing biblical immorality, injustice, and inequality to pursue social equity under the guise of so-called justice.

However, true justice must never be separated from righteousness. Every godly form of social justice attempts to influence societal norms to follow the golden rule, what the Bible calls the royal law to "love your neighbor as yourself." See Mark 12:28; Jam. 2:8; Gal. 5:14; and Rom. 13:9. Pursue fruitfulness that is both morally righteous and biblically just.

PRAYER

Heavenly Father, help me prioritize my efforts, live a fruitful life, obey Your moral law, and pursue righteousness and justice. Change me, and the world, from the inside-out. In Jesus' name. Amen.

JOURNAL

1. You're 16 days into a program I think will help you fulfill your purpose. Have you ever appreciated how you simply being morally righteous and just is a key aspect of God's purpose for you? How does awareness of this shift your perspective?

2. Does the Change Spectrum shift how you've been prioritizing your fruitfulness? Talk to God about it. What should you emphasize and focus more? What should you focus on less?

3. Where have you stood when it comes to "social justice" prior to today's lesson? Where you, generally speaking, for or against it? Were you more concerned with equality under God and under the Law, or equity? If God is concerned with equality, could Satan be the one behind these systems all about equity? Ask God, for what reasons might Satan be doing this?

Day 17

Are Good Works evidence of your Saving Faith?

All ethical people obeying their conscience recognize some need for morality and good deeds. This is why nearly every false religion teaches salvation-by-works. The idea that we can somehow earn salvation.

Christianity teaches the opposite: that we're dead in our sins and transgressions (Eph. 2:1) and can only be saved by God's grace alone, through faith alone, in Christ alone. Ephesians 2:8-10 says,

> "For it is by grace you have been saved, through faith—and this is not from yourselves, it is the gift of God—not by works, so that no one can boast. For we are God's handiwork, created in Christ Jesus to do good works, which God prepared in advance for us to do."

Our works don't help us earn salvation but that doesn't mean they don't play any role in it. They do reveal if we're repentant, obedient to God, committed to being a disciple of Jesus, born of the Holy Spirit, and actively undergoing the sanctification process.

Fruitfulness then is the evidence of genuine Saving Faith. With God's

Spirit living inside comes the fruit of His Spirit in our lives and the natural outflow of His character and will manifested in us as a result. It's in this way that we become God's handiwork capable of doing good works. Matthew 7:19 says,

> "Every tree that does not bear good fruit is cut down and thrown into the fire."

This lesson covers how to make sure your works are eternally fruitful and serve as evidence of Saving Faith.

SAVING FAITH INCLUDES HUMILITY AND MERCY

Micah 6:8 says,

> "He [God] has shown you... what is good... what does the Lord require of you? To act justly... love mercy and... walk humbly with your God."

Mercy is extending compassion or forgiveness when it's within your rights to pursue justice. Those who believe they're saved by their own good works don't fully appreciate mercy. The religions that are the most legalistic are also the ones that are most cruel because people get the punishment that they deserve.

But Christianity is built on the foundation that Jesus got the punishment that we all deserve! Without God's mercy we deserve wrath, so we're to have mercy in our hearts towards others as well. Jesus taught this in His parable of The Unforgiving Servant (Matt. 18:21-35). Verses 33-35 say,

> "Shouldn't you have had mercy on your fellow servant just as I had on you?' In anger his master handed him over to the jailers to be tortured... This is how my heavenly Father will treat each of you unless you forgive your brother or sister from your heart."

James 2:12-13 says,

> "Speak and act as those who are going to be judged by the law that gives freedom, because judgment without mercy will be shown to anyone who has not been merciful."

The greater you trust in the gospel, the more you'll appreciate mercy, and be humble and willing to extend mercy and forgiveness to others.

FAITH WITHOUT WORKS IS DEAD

Faith is like one side of a coin, with repentance of sin and desire to do good on the opposite side. We're saved by faith alone but not by a faith that is alone. James 2:17, 26 says,

> "Faith by itself, if it is not accompanied by action, is dead... faith without deeds is dead."

Any "Christian" claiming moral righteousness, church participation, Bible reading, mission, etc. to be "works" salvation, so they're rejecting it—has a false, lawless, godless faith devoid of the Holy Spirit.

FIVE WAYS TO DETERMINE IF SOMETHING TRULY IS A GOOD WORK

1. *It's Not Believed To Merit Or Assist Salvation.* If helping salvation is the reason you're doing it, not only is it not counted as a good work pleasing God, it's hindering your faith and relationship with God.

2. *It's Not A Conflict With Gospel-Centered Living.* There are secular and interfaith partnerships that help people but require believers to keep their faith in Jesus to themselves while doing it. Any work that ultimately suppresses or compromises our primary objective to share the gospel is not a good work. Don't neglect primary things to be unequally yoked with others in secondary things.

3. *It's Built On The Foundation Of Faith In Jesus.* Only good fruit on the vine has eternal significance. Jesus said, "I am the vine; you are the branches. If you remain in me and I in you, you will bear much fruit; apart from me you can do nothing." (John 15:5). Only workmanship—good deeds, projects, businesses, missions, time, community service, financial donations—built on the foundation (Jesus) will last in the final analysis. If not, it'll be burned up with nothing to show for it eternally (1 Cor. 3:10-15).

4. *It's Inspired By Godly Motivations.* It's not just what you do, but why you do it that counts. Matthew 6:1-21 Jesus said if your good works are motivated by the praise of others, you've already received your reward. If you didn't do it for God in secret to glorify Him or get closer to Him you don't get credit.

5. *It Merits Heavenly Rewards.* Salvation is a gift but some eternal rewards are earned by good works. Jesus said, "Store up for yourselves treasures in heaven." (Matt. 6:20) We're equal in status as children of God but receive different rewards based on desire, effort and merit (2 Cor. 5:10).

GOOD WORKS ARE EVIDENCE OF DISCIPLESHIP AND SANCTIFICATION

John 14:15 Jesus said,

"If you love me, you will keep my commandments." (ESV)

1 John 2:4-6 says,

"Whoever says, "I know him," but does not do what he commands is a liar... if anyone obeys his word, love for God is truly made complete in them. This is how we know we are in him: Whoever claims to live in him must live as Jesus did."

John 15:8 Jesus said,

> "Bear much fruit and so prove to be my disciples." (ESV)

Pursuing a fruitful life, in faith, also proves you're a disciple of Jesus. Good fruit, internal and external, is also evidence that you're being sanctified by the Holy Spirit. Romans 6:21-22 says,

> "What fruit were you getting at that time... the end of those things is death. But now... you have been set free from sin and have become slaves of God, the fruit you get leads to sanctification and its end, eternal life." (ESV)

Tough trials will come. You may go through seasons where you have doubts, stumble into sin, or wrestle with God over why He's allowing certain difficulties. If you're in a state of righteousness and victory, your good fruit will help give you confidence as an outward sign that you belong to Jesus and the evidence shows that.

If you begin bearing bad fruit or fall back into old sinful patterns, let this serve as an outward sign to remind you you're going in the wrong direction and need to change something.

Your fruit, both the internal and external, can be a useful guide. It's an outward reflection that you can see, of your inner spiritual condition that you can't see. Use it as your compass. It will tell you if you need to change directions.

PRAYER

Heavenly Father, help me bear good fruit inspired by godly motivations and Gospel-centered living, that is evidence of my saving faith, discipleship, and sanctification. In Jesus' name. Amen.

JOURNAL

1. Are you humble and merciful? Are you quick to forgive and extend grace? Are these ways you'd describe yourself, or how others would describe you? Reflect on this and ask God to confirm or convict, as necessary.

2. Write down a few things that you do regularly that you would consider a good work you do because you're a Christian.

3. Go back to the list of "five ways to determine if something is a good work" list. Examine it carefully. Should you make adjustments in either the activity or the motive and posture of your heart in the activity?

Day 18

The Christian Mission is Not to Fix the World

Do you feed the poor, help the sick, or fight injustices? Are these your "Christian mission" activities? These things are good fruit but they're not the primary purpose, mission, or goal of the church.

What is? Preach the gospel and make disciples! This lesson we'll look at the bigger picture and examine several reasons why fixing the world is not our mission as Christians.

GOOD FRUIT IS ONLY THE BYPRODUCT

Christians must bear good fruit. This is what we were created to do (Eph. 2:10), and every tree that doesn't bear good fruit will be destroyed (Matt. 7:19). Nonetheless, this is not why the church exists, nor is it our mission as disciples of Jesus.

For example, it's not our job to eradicate poverty. Yes, it's good to feed or help the poor, but Jesus also said in John 12:8,

> *"You will always have the poor among you."*

DAY 18 - THE CHRISTIAN MISSION IS NOT TO FIX THE WORLD

It's not our job to make the world Christian or to eradicate all sin and injustice. It's certainly good when we're able to influence towards this end, that is part of us helping to advance the Kingdom of God. However, Jesus did say in Revelation 22:11,

> "Let the one who does wrong continue to do wrong; let the vile person continue to be vile; let the one who does right continue to do right; and let the holy person continue to be holy."

Not only is there an absence of commands in the Bible to focus on fixing those kinds of things, it's the exact opposite. Jesus explicitly commands us not to concern ourselves with trying to fix them. He also warned in Matthew 24 that regardless of the good effort we help improve, the world is actually still going to continue to get worse. Jesus said there will be an increase in wickedness and spiritual coldness, as well as global wars, famines, natural disasters, false prophets, and persecution for Christians. Matthew 24:12-14 says,

> "Because of the increase of wickedness, the love of most will grow cold, but the one who stands firm to the end will be saved. And this gospel of the kingdom will be preached in the whole world as a testimony to all nations, and then the end will come."

What does Jesus want us to do? Persevere in the faith and preach the gospel.

THIS WORLD ISN'T YOUR HOME

Another reason it's not our job to fix the world is 1 Cor. 7:31 says not to be consumed in the things of this world, because in its present form is passing away. 1 John 2:15-17 contrasts the world with God even bolder saying,

> "Do not love the world or anything in the world. If anyone loves the world, love for the Father is not in them. For everything in the world—the lust of the flesh, the lust of the eyes, and the pride of life—comes not from

the Father but from the world. The world and its desires pass away, but whoever does the will of God lives forever."

The Church is the holy "called-out" ones, who are no longer of this world. We've been spiritually born again, adopted by God, and are now members of His family and kingdom. Our activities shouldn't primarily be the same the secular people and organizations care about. If the unsaved, sinful world is concerned with the same social issues that's an indication that it's not the primary mission of the Church. Matthew 6:32-33 Jesus said,

"The pagans run after all these things... But seek first his [God's] kingdom and his righteousness."

Don't just feed the poor food—feed them Jesus! Jesus's prayer to the Father reveals how we should see the world and our purpose. John 17:14-23 Jesus says,

"The world has hated them, for they are not of the world any more than I am of the world... As you sent me into the world, I have sent them into the world... so that the world may believe that you have sent me... Then the world will know that you sent me and have loved them even as you have loved me."

Our mission is to help the world believe in and know Jesus.

TREASURES IN HEAVEN

God doesn't care how big your house is or how much is in your retirement plan. His primary concern is not public education, healthcare, politics, or economics. Matthew 6:19-21 Jesus said,

"Do not store up for yourselves treasures on earth, where moths and vermin destroy, and where thieves break in and steal. But store up for yourselves treasures in heaven, where moths and vermin do not destroy,

DAY 18 - THE CHRISTIAN MISSION IS NOT TO FIX THE WORLD

> *and where thieves do not break in and steal. For where your treasure is, there your heart will be also."*

Get your eyes off of the pleasures and treasures of this world! This is true even of basic necessities. Matt. 6:31 Jesus said,

> *"So do not worry, saying, 'What shall we eat?' or 'What shall we drink?' or 'What shall we wear?'"*

So focus more on the eternal, spiritual needs and outcomes. Align your objectives in the world with God's objectives. Does He want to abolish poverty? Disease? Climate change? Then He will. It's good to strengthen marriages and families, both your own and those in society. Nonetheless, like all others, even these should not be your main purpose. Jesus said in Matthew 19:29,

> *"And everyone who has left houses or brothers or sisters or father or mother or wife or children or fields for my sake will receive a hundred times as much and will inherit eternal life."*

Remember the long term goal of why God created humanity: to have a people for Himself that know and enjoy Him for eternity. For this to happen, Jesus and the gospel must permeate the hearts and minds of people. This is eternally significant, but it might not bear fruit from a worldly perspective immediately or perhaps even at all. Everything that is temporary needs to become secondary and take the back seat.

GOD'S FRUIT CAN BE PERCEIVED AS BAD FRUIT

Fortunately, many of the good, fruitful things that we do as Christians will be seen by the rest of the unsaved w1orld as good to them, too. People usually won't fault you for a strong marriage, raising children with morals and manners, advocacy for justice or equality, praying for the sick, serving the vulnerable, helping the poor, animals, etc. We should definitely celebrate the fact that we agree on this with unbelievers and take advantage of it.

But this won't always be the case. When we shift our perspective of what's fruitful according to God, it IS going to be different than what's fruitful according to the world. God's way may seem bad, unkind, or unloving, to those still in rebellion to Him. If the world doesn't dislike what you're doing, at least a little, you're not preaching that people are sinners that need to repent, and Jesus is the only way to avoid Hell! Because this will be offensive to people still living in sin.

When you don't participate in the same sinful activities, drunkenness, cursing, gossip or greed, and you use your wealth to advance God's Kingdom rather than hoarding it for yourself to live a lavish worldly life just like them, they'll feel convicted. Your life should be marked by being noticeably different from of unbelievers. This is part of your true mission.

PRAYER

Heavenly Father, help me to remember this world isn't my home and prioritize my primary mission to preach the gospel, make disciples, and store up treasures in Heaven. In Jesus' name. Amen.

JOURNAL

1. Ask God to remind you of time you've spent in "mission" activities that had zero to do with sharing the gospel, making disciples. What will you do differently in the future?

2. While there are plenty of "innocent-enough" things in this world to enjoy, it's still largely sinful. Ask God what areas of your life or heart still have too much love for, or attachment to, this world and the things in it. Discuss how to change this.

3. If not already true, at some point your society will hate you for taking a firm stand as a follower of Jesus. How will you respond? How could you store up more eternal treasures?

Day 19

Your Mission as a Disciple of Jesus

Fixing the world is not your mission as a disciple of Jesus. What is? Your mission is to live here like a spiritual alien on a foreign planet. This lesson covers four parts:

1. Being a light in the world
2. Preaching the gospel
3. Making disciples
4. Advancing God's kingdom

BE A LIGHT IN THE WORLD

There's two spiritual kingdoms: Satan's and God's. Satan is the prince of this world having authority over those held captive by sin and death (Heb. 2:14-15). But Jesus has all authority in heaven and on earth (Matt. 28:18). Jesus was revealed to destroy the works of the devil (1 John 3:8), and He reigns with all dominion, power, and authority (Eph. 1:20-22; 1 Cor. 15:23-27). Matt. 16:18 Jesus said,

> *"I will build my church, and the gates of Hades will not overcome it."*

Luke 10:17-19 says,

> *"Lord, even the demons submit to us in your name... [Jesus responded] I have given you authority to trample on snakes and scorpions and to overcome all the power of the enemy; nothing will harm you."*

You've been justified by faith and given the Holy Spirit, supernatural empowerment, and spiritual gifts to have victory over sin and help others encounter God through you.

Phil. 2:14-15 it says you've been given the ability to,

> *"become blameless and pure, "children of God without fault in a warped and crooked generation." Then you will shine among them like stars in the sky."*

Your mission is to be holy, righteous and godly! Matt. 5:14-16 Jesus said,

> *"You are the light of the world... let your light shine before others, that they may see your good deeds and glorify your Father in heaven."*

PREACH THE GOSPEL

Mark 16:15 Jesus said,

> *"Go into all the world and preach the gospel to all creation."*

Some people quote St. Francis of Assisi saying, "Preach the Gospel at all times, when necessary, use words." This is nonsense. It's like saying, "Teach students the ABC's, when necessary, use letters." The gospel needs words; it's a message to a person from their Creator. Romans 10:14-15 says,

> *"How... can they call on the one they have not believed in?... how can*

> they believe in the one of whom they have not heard?... how can they hear without someone preaching to them?... "How beautiful are the feet of those who bring good news!"

You can reinforce the gospel by having love, character, and good deeds with it, but you can't leave out the message. 2 Cor. 5:19-20 says,

> "[God] has committed to us the message of reconciliation. We are therefore Christ's ambassadors, as though God were making his appeal through us."

You're a letter messenger. You can't control if they'll accept God's invitation or throw it in the trash. All you can do is to deliver it, then it's on them. Matt. 22:8-9 Jesus said,

> "The wedding banquet is ready... go to the street corners and invite to the banquet anyone you find."

Acts 1:8 Jesus said,

> "You will be my witnesses in Jerusalem, and in all Judea and Samaria, and to the ends of the earth."

Your mission is to be His witness and verbally share the Gospel to those within your influence.

MAKE DISCIPLES THAT MAKE DISCIPLES

Matthew 28:19-20 Jesus said,

> "Go and make disciples of all nations... teaching them to obey everything I have commanded you."

The ultimate goal of preaching the gospel and congregating with believers, is to make disciples. A disciple of Jesus is a convinced and committed adherent, who knows, follows, and obeys Him. Discipleship isn't a program to complete, but a process to become, more like Jesus. You can't force people to be like Him, but you can first model it and then teach it to those who are interested.

"Go and make disciples" is a command. Some interpret this saying, "as you are going, make disciples." In the former, the reason we're going is to make disciples, i.e. The Great Commission. In the latter, we're going for whatever reason of our own perhaps making disciples on the way. It's a good thing if they mean we should be witnessing and discipling everywhere. But it's a huge problem if the aim of this interpretation is to make it seem less religious or works-based —less like it's not our primary purpose and mission!

As though Jesus intends for us to go about our lives however we feel like as long as we're trying to make disciples on the way. That's living for ourselves first. As though Jesus's ministry didn't model intentionally going to new villages to proclaim the gospel and make disciples. As though the early church didn't model intentionally going to new cities to proclaim the gospel and make disciples. If we're choosing the primary direction we're going, with making disciples as a secondary thing we add-in when convenient, that's backwards. Jesus said in Luke 14:26-33,

> *"If anyone comes to me and does not hate father and mother, wife and children, brothers and sisters—yes, even their own life—such a person cannot be my disciple. And whoever does not carry their cross and follow me cannot be my disciple... those of you who do not give up everything you have cannot be my disciples."*

The Holy Spirit is to lead. We're dead to ourselves and live for Christ. Make disciples as you're going—also—but first and foremost, intentionally go and make disciples and live on that mission.

DAY 19 - YOUR MISSION AS A DISCIPLE OF JESUS

ADVANCE THE KINGDOM OF GOD

By this I do not mean try to fix the world, convert the world, take over all the governments of the world, or subdue the world in any way that makes it necessary or helpful to usher in Jesus's return. I make a point to say all of that because some ministries do actually teach that. This is connected with what is called Kingdom Now theology, Dominion theology, postmillennialism—no—I see no biblical evidence for believing that any of these things are true or that the Church will be used somehow to save the world.

Jesus warned in Matthew 24, regardless of the good we help to influence, the world is going to get WORSE. There will be an increase in wickedness, wars, famines, natural disasters, false prophets, and persecution. Matthew 24:12-14 says,

> *"Because of the increase of wickedness, the love of most will grow cold, but the one who stands firm to the end will be saved. And this gospel of the kingdom will be preached in the whole world as a testimony to all nations, and then the end will come."*

He goes on to say in verses 19-21,

> *"How dreadful it will be in those days... For then there will be great distress, unequaled from the beginning of the world until now—and never to be equaled again."*

The Kingdom of God is everyone and everything under God's dominion; all He's King over. Satan is governing sin on earth without God's endorsement. We're to seek what Jesus says to pray in Matthew 6:10,

> *"Our Father in heaven, hallowed be your name, your kingdom come, your will be done, on earth as it is in heaven."*

This is a request to God of what we want Him to do, not a mandate from God of what He wants us to do. Your mission is to advance God's spiritual dominion everywhere you're able to. And the WAY that we do that is by being a light in a dark world, preaching the gospel, and making disciples.

PRAYER

Heavenly Father, help me to have victory over all sin and shine as a radiant light in this dark world, preach the gospel, make disciples, and advance Your kingdom on earth. In Jesus' name. Amen.

JOURNAL

1. Have you felt aimless? Do you now understand what your calling and purpose are? Are you ready to answer that call today?! Talk to God about how you feel about these things.

2. These four items are meant to be general things we are all to do. However, for the sake of this assignment, which one of the four do you feel the most passionate about? Discuss with God why you think this is so.

3. Have you ever walked up to a total stranger in a public place and verbally shared the gospel message with them? Close your eyes and take a few moments right now to do it in your imagination. Have the entire conversation including how they could respond.

Day 20

4 Keys to Run your Spiritual Race well

Hebrews 12:1-2 says,

> *"Let us throw off everything that hinders and the sin that so easily entangles. And let us run with perseverance the race marked out for us, fixing our eyes on Jesus, the pioneer and perfecter of faith."*

This lesson we'll examine four ways to do this:

1. Embracing your role as a good steward
2. Storing up eternal rewards
3. Embracing endurance through tribulation
4. Embracing perseverance for a refined faith

EMBRACE YOUR ROLE AS A GOOD STEWARD

Your life isn't your own. You're a manager of it for God. You're to be a good, faithful steward over everything God has entrusted you with. In the Parable of the Talents (Matthew 25:14-30) Jesus teaches what He expects from His disciples when He leaves them in charge.

The master went out of town and left each of his three servants talents (a measure of money) to steward for him. Two of them invested theirs and doubled the master's money, the third buried his in the ground. When the master returned he praised the first two. He called them good and faithful, rewards and promotes them, and then welcomes them into his joy.

But the third servant he doesn't call less good, but wicked and lazy! His portion was taken from him and then he was thrown into the outer darkness, language elsewhere described as Hell!

You have been entrusted with many things belonging to the Lord and you're responsible for how you steward them. It isn't only your money, it's also your spiritual gifts, abilities, personality, experiences, roles, votes, influence, etc. Everything you are, how you lived, and what you did with all of your life!

Jesus shows the same opportunity being received by two different types of servants. The first two love and trust their master, and because of that they care about what He cares about. They felt entrusted to get this responsibility, and they were eager to please Him.

The third servant hated, distrusted, blamed, and even slandered the character of his master. He felt fearful to have this responsibility, was self-centered, and neglected to do anything good with what was entrusted to him.

Be a good steward. Run the race so that you're rewarded at the end.

STORE UP ETERNAL REWARDS

There are two judgment events. The first is the great white throne judgment where all appear at the resurrection. Some will receive eternal life, others eternal damnation. See Matt. 25:32; Rev. 20:11-15. Romans 2:16 calls it,

> *"the day when God judges people's secrets through Jesus Christ."*

1 John 2:28 says,

> "continue in him [Christ], so that when he appears we may be confident and unashamed before him at his coming."

But there's also a second judgment for all of the saved, called the Bema Judgment, where we receive eternal rewards based on our performance as a Christian this life. 2 Corinthians 5:10 calls it,

> "the judgment seat of Christ, so that each of us may receive what is due us for the things done while in the body, whether good or bad."

Run the race to be rewarded later for good stewardship, not ashamed for all you could've done and didn't. Romans 14:10-13 says,

> "For we will all stand before God's judgment seat... each of us will give an account of ourselves to God. Therefore let us stop passing judgment on one another. Instead, make up your mind not to put any stumbling block or obstacle in the way of a brother or sister."

Strive to be a positive influence on how your brothers and sisters in Christ do there too. Luke 14:14 Jesus said,

> "you will be repaid at the resurrection of the righteous."

Colossians 3:23-24 says,

> "Whatever you do, work at it with all your heart, as working for the Lord, not for human masters, since you know that you will receive an inheritance from the Lord as a reward. It is the Lord Christ you are serving. Anyone who does wrong will be repaid for their wrongs, and there is no favoritism."

EMBRACE ENDURANCE THROUGH TRIBULATION

This journey is a marathon, not a sprint. Endurance is an important part of your race not to underestimate. Many have faced religious persecution for Jesus since the first century.

I don't wish this for any of us, but in a weird way there's a blessing to it. For those who have endured rather than forsake Jesus in their moment of trial, their faith was tested in the fire and shown approved. They may have more confidence in their faith than those who've not yet had a major testing.

By facing martyrdom, or merely living persecuted, they're continually earning treasures in Heaven. Imagine that, earning rewards just for dying or living! Perhaps the world may bring tribulation to you, or perhaps you will invite it by living intentionally on mission for Jesus and pursue a less comfortable life.

Many will endure what the Bible calls the Great Tribulation, the final few years before Jesus returns. Revelation 13:10 says,

> *"This calls for patient endurance and faithfulness on the part of God's people."*

This is a final refining fire to test the world before the end. For the Church, it's our final test of perseverance, and last opportunity to witness for Jesus.

But it's not just this final generation that goes through tribulation. Every generation does. We're all called to endure whatever the Lord allows us to go through. Perseverance is a demonstration of your faith in Jesus, and part of your calling. Revelation 7:9-17 shows this and our reward:

> *"There before me was a great multitude that no one could count, from every nation, tribe, people and language, standing before the throne and before the Lamb... These are they who have come out of the great tribulation; they have washed their robes and made them white in the blood of the Lamb... 'Never again will they hunger; never again will they thirst... God will wipe away every tear from their eyes.'"*

EMBRACE PERSEVERANCE FOR A REFINED FAITH

Knowing that we will endure tribulation is different than knowing why we will, as in the purpose and benefit of it. Our perseverance refines our faith and confirms our salvation. Paul reminds us in Romans 5:3-5 to rejoice in our tribulation and he tells the benefits of it:

> *"We also glory in our sufferings, because we know that suffering produces perseverance; perseverance, character; and character, hope. And hope does not put us to shame, because God's love has been poured out into our hearts through the Holy Spirit, who has been given to us."*

Your perseverance, through faith in Jesus, is what shows you approved. It's not that enduring any type of suffering is good, but when it is good whenever it is a demonstration of your faith in Jesus through tribulation. 1 Peter 4:12 says,

> *"Do not be surprised at the fiery ordeal that has come on you to test you, as though something strange were happening to you."*

For more on suffering for being a Christian read verses 12-19. Additionally, Colossians 1:23 says, we've been reconciled through Jesus and made holy,

> *"if you continue in your faith, established and firm, and do not move from the hope held out in the gospel."*

The refining fire of tribulation tests what we're made of, like a blazing fire consuming a piece of coal. It's our faith in Jesus that enables us to persevere through the fire and pressure and then come out like a diamond!

PRAYER

Heavenly Father, help me throw off every sin and comfort that hinders and run my race well. Help me be a good steward, store up eternal treasures, endure and persevere. In Jesus' name. Amen.

JOURNAL

1. Pray and ask God to reveal to you and give you understanding about how you could be a better steward of what He has entrusted you with. Ask Him for specific actions that you could take today.

2. Have you experienced persecution or tribulation as a result of following Jesus? Are you ready to? Ask God to search your heart and confirm your commitment to even suffer and die for Jesus.

3. If/when you go through persecution will you just blame political parties, government, foreign policy, greedy corporations, racism, woke ideologies, religion, terrorism, or one of a million other things—or will you blame sin? Will you remember to let who you're blaming keep you USING that difficult to test and refine your faith and show it approved? Or will you waste the opportunity to complain about the world. Role play it in your imagination. Ask the Holy Spirit to help you examine your heart and talk with God about it.

Day 21

Who and What is The Church?

What is the church? Is it simply any building with a cross on it? Is it all who believe and follow Jesus globally? Is it that Roman Catholic organization that Jesus gave all authority to through the Apostle Peter? Is there any truth to that claim? What does it mean to be the Bride or Body of Christ? This lesson we'll explore all of these things and exactly who and what the church is.

WHAT THE WORD CHURCH MEANS

The original Greek word we translate in English to "church" is ekklésia (ek-klay-see'-ah) which meant an assembly or congregation. It isn't a direct translation, ekklésia could've been any kind of assembly, not only a Christian one, or even a religious gathering. It originally comes from the Greek words ek, meaning "out from and to" and kaléo (kah-lay-oh), meaning "to call."

The Christianized interpretation of this is that people are called out from the world, and towards God, with the outcome of them now being distinctly separate from those still spiritually dead and lost within the world. Since the Greek word for "Lord" is kyrios (kee-ree-ohs), which is what the disciples called Jesus, our English word church comes from the Greek word kyriakos (kee-ree-ah-kos), meaning "belonging to the Lord." Thus, the English word "church" refers to any assembly of people who belong to Jesus.

THE ROMAN CATHOLIC CHURCH IS NOT JESUS'S CHURCH

This organization claims to be the one true church with divine authority to pronounce what's true and false, declaring Christians disagreeing with them as either heretics or estranged brethren not in communion with Jesus's one true established church.

Their claim to supreme authority as Jesus's official representative, through their magisterium, pope, and bishops in union with the pope, dates not to the 1st century, when Jesus lived, but to the 6th century.

Their claim to sole authority and only accurate interpreter of the Bible, is their basis for introducing doctrines that seemingly and often outright contradict the Bible. These include the worship and intercession of Mary and deceased saints, Catholic sacramental and penitential system, salvation by works, purgatory, indulgences, religious wars, etc.

Their entire edifice is based on a single statement that is found in Matthew 16:15-19. It says,

> "But what about you?" Jesus asked. "Who do you say I am?" Simon Peter answered, "You are the Christ, the Son of the living God." Jesus replied, "Blessed are you, Simon son of Jonah! For this was not revealed to you by flesh and blood, but by My Father in heaven. And I tell you that you are Peter, and on this rock I will build My church, and the gates of Hades will not prevail against it. I will give you the keys of the kingdom of heaven. Whatever you bind on earth will be bound in heaven, and whatever you loose on earth will be loosed in heaven."

Jesus didn't establish His church on Peter, who He called Satan four verses later, nor an authoritarian role given to him. Jesus did not want a religious dictatorship (Matt. 20:24-28, 23:5-12, 18:1-4; Eph. 4:11-17).

"This rock" was Peter's profession of faith, inspired by the Father, that Jesus is the eternal Son of God, that His church is built on. Jesus simply did a play on words since they were standing on a rock cliff and Peter's nickname Petros meant pebble.

None of the apostles, including Peter, believed Jesus gave Peter authority or that that part of what Jesus said was even significant. They argued afterwards about who was greatest (Luke 22:24). The same event and speech is also recorded in Mark 8:27-30 and Luke 9:18-20. Neither one of those accounts thought Jesus's comments to Peter about him being the rock, getting the keys, binding and loosing, etc. even worth mentioning!

Mark's gospel was even written from Rome with Peter to give Peter's perspective so it's really telling that Mark's gospel leaves it out! Jesus didn't give only Peter the keys. He gave all the apostles the keys explicitly in Matt. 18:15-20. In fact, He gave all disciples the keys (1 Cor. 3:22).

Peter later wrote in his letter that it is faith in Jesus, not himself, that is the rock and foundation (1 Pet. 2:4-8). Peter liked the rock metaphor but he didn't falsely believe that he was the leader of the entire church. And if he wasn't we certainly shouldn't blindly accept the Roman Catholic Church's baseless claim that every future bishop of the city Peter happened to die in (Rome) automatically becomes the sole leader of the entire Church. So, no, there is no basis for believing this claim or any of the unbiblical doctrines they've introduced since then.

THE GLOBAL CAPITAL "C" CHURCH

The church is not an administrative religious organization, nor is it buildings. It is every individual that has been born again by the Spirit of God. It's all people, everywhere, any time in history, who belong to Jesus. It's these whom "the gates of Hades will not overcome." Hades is the realm of the dead. The church is all who've had their sins forgiven, been spiritually reborn, and passed from death to life (1 John 3:14).

The true Church is spiritual. Only God knows who is truly in it, because you must be born of His Spirit to be in it. Even if every single public gathering in the world was disbanded, every church building torn down, and every Christian isolated in their home, there would still be a global, universal, spiritual Church visible to God. Acts 20:28 says,

> *"Keep watch over yourselves and all the flock of which the Holy Spirit has made you overseers. Be shepherds of the church of God, which he bought with his own blood."*

The Global Church is referred often as the Bride of Christ. This beautiful metaphor emphasizes individuals belonging to Jesus while also united together collectively in a special eternal covenant relationship (2 Cor. 11:2; Matt. 9:14-16; John 3:28-30). Revelation 19:6-7 says,

> *"God Almighty reigns… give him glory! For the wedding of the Lamb has come, and his bride has made herself ready."*

THE BODY OF CHRIST

When born of the Holy Spirit, we're baptized into one Spirit, submerged into Christ's spiritual body (Col. 1:24; 1 Cor. 12; Rom. 12). This metaphor shows how we're an integrated spiritual whole. As an individual body part, it captures our unique individuality, calling, and purpose, as a Body, a larger whole with a common calling and purpose.

There should be no division in the body but care and concern for one another. The Holy Spirit hasn't given any one part everything they need alone, and no part is greater than the others. Each is given a certain portion so that in the unified whole the fullness of Christ is realized. All this points to the relational aspects of the Holy Trinity, and God's desire for us to become a family. Ephesians 5:23-27 says,

> *"Christ is the head of the church, his body, of which he is the Savior… the church submits to Christ… just as Christ loved the church and gave himself up for her to make her holy, cleansing her by the washing with water through the word, and to present her to himself as a radiant church, without stain or wrinkle or any other blemish, but holy and blameless."*

THE LOCAL CONGREGATION

This is the physical, visible expression of the "true Church" of Jesus, which is spiritual and invisible. This is where the capital C Church is shown to the world. Where people are called out of the world to somewhere else distinct, meetings for people who believe in and follow Jesus.

Paul calls congregations and the individuals in them the church (1 Cor. 16:19). This is where believers meet to worship Jesus together, unite in common mission, and support, encourage, and serve one another in love (Heb. 10:24-25).

PRAYER

Lord Jesus, help me embrace being a member of Your Global Church, Your Bride and Body, and not forsake assembling together in unity and service with other believers. In Jesus' name. Amen.

JOURNAL

1. Do you feel connected to the global Church? Spiritually you are. Pray for the world's currently 100 million persecuted Christians, and for the families and communities of the world's 150,000 martyrs currently murdered annually simply because they belong to Jesus. Ask the Lord to share His heart about this with you.

2. Have you had hatred or unforgiveness against other Christian denominations, groups, or churches? (I'm not talking about hating false teachings but people). Pray for unity for the Body of Christ, everyone that has been born again. Pray that error would be exposed and truth discovered. Pray that Jesus's Bride would become radiant, without stain or wrinkle but holy and blameless. Talk with God about His Church.

Day 22

What are the Basic Functions of the Local Church?

Is being part of a church optional? Hebrews 10:24-25 says,

> *"Let us consider how we may spur one another on toward love and good deeds, not giving up meeting together, as some are in the habit of doing, but encouraging one another- and all the more as you see the Day approaching."*

Church participation isn't optional. It's both a biblical command and essential for personal growth, life purpose and optimal fulfillment. This lesson we'll explore several basic functions of the local church.

CHRIST-CENTERED COMMUNITY

It's very easy to be influenced and persuaded by who and what we're around on a regular basis. An interesting fact is that people usually earn an income equivalent to the average income of the five people they spend the most time with. When a person's closest companions are unbelievers, have unbiblical beliefs, or live immorally, they will influence them to think

DAY 22 - WHAT ARE THE BASIC FUNCTIONS OF THE LOCAL CHURCH?

and live the same way (2 Cor. 6:14-18).

Regular church gatherings can help members remember we've been called out from a lost, sinful world. We now belong to God's family and kingdom. There are many unique aspects of this diverse community united around a common interest: Jesus.

One is the embrace of a *Christian Identity and Worldview*. It's important to regularly renew our commitment to live holy, set apart lives that are very different from the standards of those in the world. It's important to gather together with others also committed to this same objective to help one another continue to be renewed in our thinking, beliefs, and worldview.

Another is *Corporate Worship*. This activity foreshadows Heaven itself, people worshipping God, united together in Spirit, encountering His presence both individually and corporately. This is often some form of music and singing but can also include dancing, flag twirling, shouting, corporate prayer, corporate devotional time, or other creative expressions of worship.

Then there's *Fellowship* which is any social gathering for the purpose of building community bonds. Many churches will have communal meals, recreational outings, social events, worship concerts, theatrical plays, games, sports, or other activities. The idea is that they're all done in the presence and Spirit of the Lord with the goal of helping members form a sense of corporate belonging and build relationships.

Then there's *Sacraments* which are sacred rites instituted by Christ for His church to do as visible symbols of divine acts. Baptism is a ceremony where members of the church initiate a new believer into Jesus' Church by immersing them in water as a public demonstration of their faith in Jesus as Lord and Savior and their decision to follow Him (Matt. 28:19; Acts 2:37-38). The Lord's Supper is a ceremony where generally already-baptized believers eat bread and juice, presented as a thanks offering and memorial, for spiritual communion with the body and blood of Christ (Luke 22:14-23; 1 Cor. 11:26).

TRAINING TO THINK AND LIVE BIBLICALLY

A very important function of the local church is to preach and teach from God's Word, the Bible. Knowing and living according to the biblical standards is paramount. Romans 15:4 says,

> *"Everything... was written to teach us, so that through the endurance taught in the Scriptures and the encouragement they provide we might have hope."*

In Acts 6:2-4 the early church records,

> *"The Twelve gathered all the disciples together and said, "It would not be right for us to neglect the ministry of the word of God... [we] will give our attention to prayer and the ministry of the word."*

The Bible is provided to sanctify us (John 17:17), make us wise (Ps. 19:7), help us believe (John 20:31), guide us (Ps. 119:9), and give us spiritual life (Matt. 4:4). In the past the role of teaching God's Word was even more significant than it is today because very few people had copies themselves.

With the invention of the printing press and then the Protestant Reformation people began to read the Bible for themselves. This was good and it exposed many false Catholic teachings that people had just assumed were the right things to believe.

However, one consequence of many people reading the Bible themselves was that it also opened the door to a surplus of new false teachings. The need for wise, godly, knowledgeable teachers became even more important to ensure that Christians were using sound biblical interpretation and establishing right beliefs and practices. Paul taught leaders this in 1 Tim. 4:13-16,

> *"Devote yourself to the public reading of Scripture, to preaching and to teaching... Be diligent in these matters... Watch your life and doctrine closely. Persevere in them, because if you do, you will save both yourself and your hearers."*

This is a primary function of the church. Gatherings led by Holy Spirit-filled, spiritually-mature, godly, wise, and theologically-trained pastors and teachers help members understand the Bible and live consistent with it.

CHRIST-CENTERED SERVICE

Allow me to return briefly to my "Road Map" car metaphor for a moment. Car enthusiasts take pride in their car, keeping it in pristine condition, upgrade its parts, and regularly service and tune it for optimal performance.

Others just see their car as a commodity. They're content if it stays in one piece and gets them from point A to point B. They give little attention to it unless it breaks and they're forced to take it to the mechanic. And then they opt for the easiest cheapest way to get it running again perhaps without concern for the best long-term care approach.

Some treat their faith this way. They don't think about Jesus, the Bible, their personal relationship with God, the church, or the spiritual purpose of their life until something breaks. When there is a financial, health, or marriage crisis, or there's a job loss, death of a loved one, or some catastrophic event happens, that's when the church then seems relevant.

It's unfortunate, but true, that for some, church only serves as a way to maintain bare-minimum spiritual requirements or get help during crises. While far from optimal, or even necessarily ensuring that they are actually saved, this type of sporadic church involvement may be enough to sustain a nominal faith, keeping it from completely derailing into nothing at all.

The regular gathering of the church as a fixed staple in a community provides a place for these kinds of people when they are seeking help. If the church is the Christ-centered community it should be, they can help them also learn how to be proactive, submit their whole lives to God, grow in Christian community, and prevent future problems from occurring.

Christians aren't to be occasional visitors nor regular spectators. We are all meant to do works of service and build one another up in love, until we all reach unity in the faith, become mature, and become like Jesus, as each does its work (Eph. 4:11-16). Church gatherings help members participate and serve one another this way. They also help members be united in a common vision and mission and thus be more collaborative and fruitful in ministry service to their neighbors. 1 Timothy 3:15 says,

> *"[We are] God's household, which is the church of the living God, the pillar and foundation of the truth."*

Titus 2:13-14 says,

> *"Our great God and Savior, Jesus Christ, who gave himself for us to redeem us from all wickedness and to purify for himself a people that are his very own, eager to do what is good."*

PRAYER

Lord Jesus, help me fully embrace Your Church in community, participating, serving, giving, fellowshipping, and building up others in love until we all become more like You. In Jesus' name. Amen.

JOURNAL

1. Are you an actively-serving, fully-contributing member of a local, Bible-believing church? If not, why not? Talk with God about it. Ask Him to heal any church hurt you have and help you forgive, move forward, and get rooted somewhere.

2. Is your church healthy? Are they actively doing these things? If so, are you involved? If not, how you could help influence it?

3. Are you part of a small group that focuses on these things? Host a group connected to your church, or if they don't have them consider starting your own independent home church, or discipleship group. This is a good ways to make disciples. You could use this book or our resources to help. Ask God how He wants you to be more involved in some type of local church.

Day 23

How to go from Healthy to Empowered Church

Want to be part of an empowered church? This lesson you'll learn what things you should be prioritizing. This applies to various aspects of traditional churches as well as ministries, home churches, and small groups.

First things first, are you doing the fundamentals? This is necessary in order to be a healthy church. Are you cultivating a Christ-centered community with members embracing a Christian identity and worldview, baptism, Lord's Supper, prayer, corporate worship, and relationship-building? Are people thinking and living biblically? Are they not just occasionally visiting or watching online? Have they moved from just spectating to actual participation and involvement (Heb. 10:24-25)?

Start with these things! Ephesians 4:11-16 teaches that we're all to do the works of the ministry and build one another up in love, until we all reach unity in the faith, and become mature and more like Jesus, as each does their work. These are the signs of a healthy church doing what they're supposed to do.

This lesson we'll explore how to go from being a simply healthy church to a truly empowered church by moving: 1) from community to family, 2) from maintenance to transformation, and 3) from participation to collaboration.

FROM COMMUNITY TO FAMILY

The more you help other members relate to and love one another as a family the more they will flourish. Many think of love as an emotion, a feeling you either have or don't. This isn't biblical. Agape love is sacrificial. It's an action you do that costs you something.

God didn't just say He loves us, or that He would do anything for us. He tangibly demonstrated His love for us, by extending grace, coming to earth, bearing the weight of our sins, and dying for us on a cross. 1 John 4:10 says,

> "This is love: not that we loved God, but that he loved us and sent his Son as an atoning sacrifice for our sins."

1 John 4:19 says,

> "We love because he first loved us."

Few churches have the intimacy and love I believe Jesus desires that we all have. Old Testament law already said to love your neighbor as yourself, but Jesus calls us to an even higher standard: to be family, loving our brothers and sisters sacrificially. John 15:12-13 He said,

> "Love each other as I have loved you. Greater love has no one than this: to lay down one's life for one's friends."

He even said our love for one another shows if we're truly disciples. John 13:34-35 says,

> "As I have loved you, so you must love one another. By this everyone will know that you are my disciples, if you love one another."

The early church modeled this. Acts 4:32-34 says,

> "All the believers were one in heart and mind. No one claimed that any of their possessions was their own, but they shared everything... God's grace was so powerfully at work in them all that there were no needy persons among them."

Help model, disciple, and train other members to more deliberately involve themselves in one another's lives. To disciple and love one another by listening to, praying for, encouraging, helping, serving, counseling, or blessing them in whatever ways they're able.

If you're in a position of leadership or influence in your church, teach others why they need to love one another, understand how to do so practically, set this as your church's cultural standard, model it from the top down, and train them to actually practice loving one another through gathering activities.

FROM MAINTENANCE TO TRANSFORMATION

It's God's will and plan to transform us into the likeness of Christ. The new covenant is for this purpose. We're justified by faith alone rather than perfection to external Laws, this gives the freedom to be led by the Spirit to focus on the things that matter most to God. Additionally, the Holy Spirit is now living within us to supernaturally deliver, sanctify, and empower us to be more like God in so many other ways. Still, many act like Christianity is just like one more religion option to choose from!

No, we as the Church are in the new spiritual creation, total life restoration and transformation business! We have a high calling, so don't settle. Not in your own life or in the lives of the people in your church. Your church should have supernaturally high standards and always be seeking to elevate everyone to continue progressing until they're living up to their highest potential.

We can have freedom from every demonic hindrance, and have victory over every sin, limiting belief, addiction, destructive habit, or toxic relationship. We can be biblically knowledgeable, emotionally healthy and whole, mentally resilient, disciplined, wise, well-balanced, and spiritually mature. We can be Spirit-led, bearing both the fruit and the mighty gifts of the Spirit. We can be disciples with rightly prioritized lives truly fulfilling our callings.

Let these things be your expectation. Trust that God is working and able to do all things. Be hopeful; be optimistic.

Many churches have the mindset that they do need to expand and continue to invite unbelievers and lost and hurting people. There's a saying: the church isn't a museum for religious people but a hospital for broken people. There's some truth to that. But notice also that people go to hospitals to get healed. Church needs to be the same way. If we bring hurting people and don't focus on the healing part then we'll just have a huge gathering of broken people and people will get even more broken by continuing to gather around such people!

Have a church expansion mindset, but not at the expense of the spiritual health of the church. No sense in inviting more broken, lost people into a church already full of sick, sinful, broken people claiming to be Christians. They'll all just keep getting worse. The health of your church should always be first priority.

You want to invite your community into a transformative relationship with Jesus through your church. They should feel God's presence, meet authentic disciples, feel real love, and know that there's something special there.

FROM PARTICIPATION TO COLLABORATION

Once your church is healthy, modeling loving family and spiritually transformed lives, you can begin shifting more focus towards outside the church's walls.

Members first learn to participate by just helping and serving where there's need. The long term goal though is to help all embrace a common vision and mission and then develop and train them to innovate and collaborate towards it. Invest in education and training programs to prepare members to become capable and competent leaders. Your core leadership needs to step back and learn to delegate and oversee. Think less teaching, more training. Teaching means to explain and educate; training means to bridge the gap from learning to being prepared to actually do the ministry work (Eph. 4:12).

Help them discover, embrace, and develop their S.H.A.P.E. and Spiritual Gifts and continue to pursue all of them. (You'll learn more about these later). The Body of Christ is being empowered with spiritual gifts for edification and expansion. Your goal should be to help bring the best out of them in ways that help them simultaneously fulfill their calling and support the mission of the church. Encourage them to work together with one another's projects as well.

There are primarily three areas to focus efforts on:

1. *Collaborative Discipleship:* The mission isn't just to get more visitors or members, it's to make disciples of Jesus who have transformed lives. Everyone should have people discipling them as well as people that they're also helping to disciple. And there should be overlap. We should be working together to all help strengthen one another.

2. *Collaborative Gospel Provision:* Bring biblical Gospel truth and God's presence to individuals or areas of society that are sinful or broken to transform them. The gospel has everything we need. We need to work together to help every person and area of society to receive all the benefits of everything that Jesus has made available to us.

3. *Collaborative Advancement:* Expand God's Kingdom, reach the lost, and advance God's spiritual dominion on earth. We need to work together in many different ways, each bringing the best that we have to offer to contribute to the benefit of the whole.

"It's not so much that God has a mission for his church in the world, but that God has a church for his mission in the world." -Christopher Wright [3]

PRAYER

Lord Jesus, help us be sacrificially loving towards our spiritual family, be transformed, and collaborate towards discipleship, gospel provision, and Kingdom advancement. In Jesus' name. Amen.

JOURNAL

1. How sacrificially loving are you? Are you modeling this well to those in your church and helping them to treat one another like family? Talk to God about it and ask Him how you can improve in this area.

2. How supernaturally transformed is your life? Is the person of Jesus and the power of the gospel being manifested in you, and are you modeling this well to those in your church and helping them to have the same? Talk to God about it and ask Him where you could improve in this area.

3. How sacrificially loving are you? Are you modeling this well to those in your church and helping them to treat one another like family? Talk to God about it and ask Him how you can improve in this area?

Day 24

What's your Identity and Calling?

Every disciple of Jesus is going to the same eternal destination but we take alternate routes to get there. Your individual life story is just one small part in God's grand narrative. Every follower of Jesus has an identical primary identity and calling. Additionally, we each also have a unique secondary identity and calling. This lesson you'll learn how to know and discover yours.

YOUR IDENTICAL PRIMARY IDENTITY AND CALLING COME FIRST

Before we get into your unique identity and calling let me make something clear. People often struggle anxiously trying to figure out their unique identity and calling. This happens because it's unclear, mysterious, debatable, and based on subjective feelings, impressions, preferences, and opinions.

However, your primary identity and calling is more important anyways! Plus, this is clear, known, unquestionable, and based on the unchanging Bible, so make sure you prioritize these. You're to always be and do these things. No excuses.

I want you to get the most out of discovering and living out your unique calling but never sacrifice your primary calling in the process.

Your unique calling is secondary and it's built on top of your primary calling as its foundation.

Included below are concepts from More by Todd Wilson and S.H.A.P.E. by Rick Warren that I have further tweaked and elaborated on.

- **BE - Core Identity.** How you were created? God created you in His image and likeness. After your new birth, your core identity is an adopted child of God the Father, the temple of the Holy Spirit, and a disciple of Jesus. Your identity further develops as you allow God's fullness to mature in you as a part of the Body and Bride of Christ.

- **DO - Core Mission.** What purpose were you made for? You were created to glorify God with your existence and know Him in relationship forever. After your new birth, your core purpose is to manifest God's presence, proclaim the gospel to all creation, make disciples of Jesus, and advance God's kingdom on earth. This doesn't change until Jesus returns.

- **GO - Core Position.** What is the mission field or position, where you're to do this? You're to do it wherever you are and wherever you happen to be whenever opportunity strikes.

YOU'RE PART OF SOMETHING LARGER THAN YOURSELF

Another truth often lost in the quest for calling is the often sinful, self-centered nature of this pursuit. A lot of this "individual calling" stuff just isn't biblical. People are so egocentric that they're convinced they're so special that God must have some prominent plan for them, often so much so that they neglect trying to meet the ordinary needs literally right in front of them!

Stop searching for the secret perfect path and find fulfillment in glorifying God, by serving others in love, meeting needs in "ordinary" ways. Become an expert at the fundamentals of the faith and helping the "one."

DAY 24 - WHAT'S YOUR IDENTITY AND CALLING?

1 Corinthians 12:12, 16-26 says,

> *"Just as a body, though one, has many parts... so it is with Christ... If the ear should say, "Because I am not an eye, I do not belong to the body," it would not for that reason stop being part of the body. If the whole body were an eye, where would the sense of hearing be?... God has placed the parts in the body... just as he wanted them to be... The eye cannot say to the hand, "I don't need you!"... On the contrary, those parts... that seem to be weaker are indispensable... God has put the body together, giving greater honor to the parts that lacked it... there should be no division in the body, but that its parts should have equal concern for each other. If one part suffers, every part suffers with it; if one part is honored, every part rejoices with it."*

We are each an equal and essential part of the Body of Christ and our core mission is to contribute to the benefit of the whole. Embrace your primary identity and calling and help others do the same. Have confidence that you're already fulfilling your calling if you're doing this.

DISCOVERING YOUR UNIQUE SECONDARY IDENTITY AND CALLING

The idea of a having a unique special way that God wants to use us can be exciting, but because of this, people tend to hyper-spiritualize it.

Some are fearful they'll get it wrong so they're always second-guessing every opportunity to serve. Others are always chasing new things and never committing to anything long term (maybe it's this? Maybe it's that?). Please rest assured that if God has a specific plan that is critical to the history of humanity, that He expects you to fulfill, He isn't going to leave it to you to figure out on your own. That's absurd.

If God did have a specific thing for you to do He'll tell you what it is, expect you to obey Him, and come alongside you and help you do it. If He's giving you time and liberty to learn, grow, discover yourself, explore your passions, and follow what the Spirit more subtly puts on your heart, praise God! If you're always seeking Him and trying to remain obedient, you'll get there.

Use the following steps to understand what He's done with you so far: who you are, how you got saved, your experiences, testimony, lessons learned, etc. These will give insights how He may use you in the future.

BE - Unique Identity. *In what ways were you uniquely created by God different from others?*

- *Values.* Your intrinsic core principles and standards of behavior. What optional, unlearned personal objectives do you consider most important? How have they shaped your life?

- *Personality.* Your distinctive personal characteristics, preferences and tendencies. How do you tend to behave, navigate life, relate to others, contribute to others, approach situations?

- *Heart.* Your desires, passions, hopes, dreams, ambitions, motivations and interests. What do you love? What unique need, activities, or social causes are you the most passionate about?

- *Abilities.* Your natural talents God gave you at birth as well as learned education, experience, or skills you've acquired in life. What ways can you uniquely glorify God and bless others?

- *Spiritual Gifts [Motivations].* These are supernatural heart desires God imparted to you when you were born again or Spirit-filled, to express His heart and love to others through you.

DO - Unique Mission. *How have you been uniquely prepared to be able to serve in unique ways?*

- *Experience.* Your testimony and the things you've gone through, good and bad, that God used to develop your faith, wisdom, etc.

You're able to help others in similar situations.

- *Spiritual Gifts [Services & Manifestations].* Holy Spirit apportions different gifts to each for a reason. The gifts you've received help indicate ways He likely wants to use you.

- *APEST or Church Roles.* Are you qualified, gifted, anointed, and passionate about an area of fivefold ministry (Eph. 4:11-16) or local church roles such as elder, deacon, director, admin?

GO - Unique Position. *How have you been uniquely positioned to serve certain people/situations?*

- *Life Roles.* Spouse, parent, child, partner, friend, citizen, voter, officer, leader? Steward it.

- *Life Situation.* Do you have access to a people group or cause you're especially able to bless?

PRAYER

Heavenly Father, help me embrace and prioritize my core identity, mission, position. Help me strengthen the Body. I trust that You are leading me through my unique calling. In Jesus' name. Amen.

JOURNAL

1. Talk with God about your primary common identity and calling. Discuss why this is more important than your unique identity and calling. Write down some things you can do to remember and embrace this truth.

2. What is your BE - Unique Identity? Ask the Lord to help you notice and appreciate the unique attributes He's given you. Answer the questions from the section above.

3. What is your DO - Unique Mission and your GO - Unique Position? Ask the Lord to help you notice and appreciate the unique gifts and experiences you've had. Answer the questions from the sections above.

Day 25

How to Be Empowered for your Mission

Yesterday we looked at how we first need to embrace our primary, common identity and calling, and what that is. After that, we're ready to pursue greater clarity from God about our unique, secondary identity and calling, and different ways to discover what that is.

Today's lesson covers the third step: identifying and planning out your life vision and mission. We'll also discuss some action principles for success.

ACTION PRINCIPLES FOR MISSION DEVELOPMENT AND ACHIEVEMENT

Pursue Presence Over Purpose.
It's better to sit at the Lord's feet, rejoicing in His presence, than to work for Him. Your missional works aren't your main purpose, knowing God is. Remember how Mary and Moses both pursued God's presence first (Luke 10:38-42; Ex. 33:12-23). Only pursue or stay in a mission that you believe God is fully behind, present, and leading you in.

Get Regular Updates.
Consistently refining your life to bear good fruit and pursue God's will and direction, help ensure you're going in the right direction. Don't just keep grinding it out using what God said or did 20 years ago. Stay flexible. Don't stubbornly persist in old plans the Spirit is no longer behind. Keep tuning in to let God keep confirming that you're still on the right track.

Focus On The Right Circles.
Most people focus too much on things outside of their control, what Stephen R. Covey calls the "Circle of Concern." This naturally will lead to fruitlessness, frustration, and depression because you have no ability to affect any of these things.

> *"Lack of direction, not lack of time, is the problem. We all have twenty-four hour days." -Zig Ziglar* [4]

Focus your time, energy, and resources on your Circle of Control, things you have control over, and on expanding your Circle of Influence, things you're able to somewhat influence. Focus on changing yourself, then your family, then church, then community. Think big but start small.

Live With Intentionality.
Sometimes God drives and He gives you specific assignments to obey and follow. But often He'll give you the wheel while whispering His will into your heart, wanting you to seek, listen, and do what you think He wants. He won't micro-manage every decision and action you make; He's trying to make you like Jesus. You need to be submissive and proactive. Be ambitious. You have a big God so have big dreams you turn into big goals! Be courageous.

> *"Intention without action is an insult to those who expect the best from you." -Andy Andrews* [5]

God put those godly desires in you and He is with you and empowering you.

Be Disciplined.

Commit to daily renewal, improvement, self-discipline, and good habit building.

> "We are what we repeatedly do. Excellence, then, is not an act but a habit." -Will Durant [6]

DEVELOPING YOUR PERSONAL LIFE VISION AND MISSION

Your Vision.

> "If you want to be happy, set a goal that commands your thoughts, liberates your energy and inspires your hopes." -Andrew Carnegie [7]

What "big godly dream" could you strive towards? I'm not talking things like get a house, become doctor, get degree, start business, get married, or have family. These may be other goals, but for your vision, think bigger!
Proverbs 19:21 says,

> "Many are the plans in a person's heart, but it is the Lord's purpose that prevails."

What is on God's heart, that He has specifically and uniquely put on your heart? If you could accomplish an ideal future outcome what would it be? Define your vision in one sentence.

Your Mission.

This is the "How?" What will you do that will help fulfill and accomplish your vision? This should be broad enough to integrate all of your primary and secondary identities and callings. Your mission will contain many goals and projects. Define it in one sentence.

DEVELOPING S.M.A.R.T. ACTION PLANS DURING YOUR MISSION

"The trouble with not having a goal is that you can spend your life running up and down the field and never score." -Bill Copeland [8]

Don't just hope, wish, and pray for your vision to happen, live consistently on mission! Do this by creating and working on actionable plans. Both small and big ambitious goals are good just be sure to break them down into smaller actionable chunks. First break goals down into SMART projects, and then break projects down into SMART milestones, and then break milestones down into SMART tasks.

- *Specific.* If your goal doesn't have both a plan and a deadline it's not a goal, it's a wish. Everything needs to be specific. Consider the 5 W's. What exactly needs to be done? Why is this important? Who is going to do it? Where is it located? When does this need to be completed by?

- *Measurable.* Everything needs to be immediately actionable and capable of being measured to quickly determine if a successful result was produced or not. This is necessary to assess your progress, meet deadlines, and keep up the excitement of getting closer to achieving your goal. Ask how much needs to be lost or gained? How will I know when this task has been completed?

- *Attainable.* Everything needs to be realistic and doable. Ambitious or challenging goals are OK as long as they're still feasible. If tasks are unattainable they won't get completed. Break down all complex or difficult tasks into smaller pieces that are easily doable. Also, address possible external constraints (people, resources, time) that would limit the ability to complete any task.

- *Relevant.* Everything needs to be meaningful to you or it won't last.

If it isn't compatible with your mission, values, needs, or desires it will eventually be abandoned. Are you the right person for this? Is this a worthwhile task to do instead of other perhaps a better or wiser alternative? Is this the right time, place, and situation for this to goal or project to be sought after right now?

- *Time-Bound.* Everything needs to have specific deadlines to help you focus your efforts. This is necessary for knowing if you're currently on track or where you are in your overall progress. Vague deadlines like sometime this year, before I'm 35, don't work. Even arbitrary deadlines—if specific, attainable, and relevant—are better and still provide motivation and accountability.

PRAYER

Heavenly Father, inspire in me a godly vision and mission I can live for, SMART action plans to achieve success towards it, and empower me to live by godly principles of action. In Jesus' name. Amen.

JOURNAL

1. Talk with God about your personal vision. Ask Him to reveal to you His highest and best will for your life. What has He given you a God-glorifying, eternally significant, passionate desire to see accomplished during your lifetime?

2. Talk with God about your personal mission. Ask Him to reveal the unique and special ways He designed you. Ask Him what natural talents, skills, and spiritual gifts and opportunities He has gifted you with? Discuss with Him what you could personally do that would help work toward your vision.

3. What is one, small, SMART step that you could commit to taking today towards your mission?

Day 26

How to Improve Your Life using TECRM

In the next few days we're going to look at different ways you can use The Empowered Christian Road Map to accomplish different objectives. First we're going to look at using this map to improve your life.

Below are three examples of common life challenges. Maybe you can relate? And if not, what areas of your life would you like to improve? Model the examples below and then fit your particular challenge in the TECRM framework. Consider how embracing these principles could provide you with direction towards God's solution.

OVERVIEW OF THE EMPOWERED CHRISTIAN ROAD MAP

1. *The Right Road Map* - All that you do moves you toward the right destination (eternal life w/ Jesus)
2. *Rebuilt and Headed In New Direction* - You're repentant, saved by grace through faith, born again
3. *Dump the Garbage Baggage* - You're dedicated to spiritual freedom, restoration and sanctification
4. *The Atmosphere In The Car* - You're renewing and managing your thoughts, beliefs and emotions
5. *The New Direction Is Fruitful* - You're dedicated to bearing more

good internal and external fruit
6. *Your Mission As Disciple* - You're embracing an eternal-minded and gospel-centered purpose
7. *The Auto Club (The Church)* - You're partnering with others in a local church in unity and purpose
8. *Same Destination, Alternate Routes* - You're embracing your unique testimony, identity and calling

Next, we'll examine three common life challenges and how applying these principles can help.

LIFE CHALLENGE #1 - DEATH OR MAJOR HEALTH CRISIS

We begin by considering the map as a whole. Can you handle death or health crises in a way that moves you towards the right destination of eternal life? Yes, we begin by not acting like those who have no hope after death, often coping with their grief by escaping with hedonism and other sinful ways. People who do this show that they love this world, fear death, and aren't trusting Jesus for eternal life (principles #1-5).

The biblical truth is that death is an unpleasant consequence of living in a fallen world, which is only fallen because of sin and rebellion to God (principles #1 and 2).

The Bible also teaches that sin and Satan can cause disease and death. This is a reminder to repent of any known sins, verbally break the curses in your family bloodline, forgive those you've held unforgiveness towards, get right with God, and pursue deliverance if you have demonic bondage (principle #3).

If you've been living in right relationship with the Lord and the enemy's still saying "God is punishing you," then rebuke him. Direct your thoughts, beliefs and emotions towards gratitude to God for giving you life at all, and saving you unto eternal life, and praise and worship Him through the trial (principle #4).

Have your church praying for you, ministering to your needs, and lay hands and pray for deliverance and healing (principle #7). Decide to view it as an opportunity to glorify Him (principles #1 and 4), bear good fruit (principle #5), be a witness for Jesus to others through it (principle #6), and if it's God's will, to even let it be part of your testimony and calling (principle #8).

LIFE CHALLENGE #2 - FEELINGS OF DEPRESSION OR ANXIETY

Now, we all go through life circumstances that shift how we feel. It's one thing to break up with someone you love and be bummed about it the rest of the weekend. It's quite another to have tormenting depression for months on end with hopelessness and suicidal thoughts.

The same is true for anxiety. It's normal to have anxiety if a lion is chasing you! It's even beneficial because you need that increased heart rate and adrenaline to think quicker and run faster. But it's quite another to have feelings of anxiety when there's no legitimate reason for it.

So it's helpful to start diagnosis by just using human reasoning to understand these things. If these feelings are reasonable and temporary then just embrace them and remind yourself they'll soon pass. But if not, let's go through the principles to diagnose.

Are you confident you have right relationship with God and eternal life (principles #1 and 2)? If you're not, that would certainly cause depression and anxiety! Start there. Perhaps getting saved solves the problem. If it doesn't, keep going.

Perhaps you have internal demonic influences causing this in the form of bad drivers, passengers, or open doors that you need deliverance and healing from (principle 3)? Start investigating these things looking for evidence of causation.

If you're close with God; living holy, sanctified, and empowered; and have no major unresolved or unhealed emotional traumas, continue to principle #4, which is about controlling your thoughts, beliefs, and emotions. Perhaps the cause of your depression or anxiety is allowing yourself to remember and focus on thoughts and beliefs that cause it?

Or, maybe you're depressed about your current life situation, or anxious because of the behavior of someone in your life? Examine these things to see if your life is bearing good fruit (principle #5).

Let your church minister to you and bond with others by sharing your struggles in small group (principle #7). Perhaps you'll be delivered, healed or counseled through it. And all these things may become a part of what deepens your relationship with God and adds to your testimony and the way that you share Jesus with others (principles #6 and 8).

LIFE CHALLENGE #3 - OVERCOMING A SINFUL HABIT

First, does God call it a sin in His Word? If so, you must forsake it. No unrepentant sinner will enter the Kingdom of God or inherit eternal life. You must decide if you trust God and want Him as your destination (principle 1).

If so, stop seeing the sin as partially OK and making excuses for yourself! Repent by seeing this sin as the death-causing, demonic bondage-producing, idolatrous lie that it is!

Stop saying you're not strong enough - you have GOD in you! You have everything you need to be victorious over sin. Humble yourself, confess your sin, deny yourself, pick up your cross, crucify the sinful flesh, and present your body as a living sacrifice holy and pleasing to God (principle 2).

Examine your life for strongholds: demonic lies and influences, limiting beliefs, unhealed traumas, bitterness, anger, etc. causing your temptations to be above average (principle 3).

Manage your thoughts (principle 4), set wise boundaries, remove ways for the enemy to tempt you or get a foothold, and develop godly habits of fruitfulness (principle 5).

Fill your life with meaning by embracing your mission as a disciple, serving your church, and living out your calling (principles 6-8).

PRAYER

Heavenly Father, cement these 8 principles in my memory. Help me use them to improve and transform my life so it makes me like Jesus and advances your Kingdom. In Jesus' name. Amen.

JOURNAL

1. What is a current life challenge that you have? If not your own challenge, perhaps you have a loved one in need of help and direction right now.

2. Is it similar to one of the example challenges provided in this lesson? How would your particular challenge fit into the TECRM framework?

3. Discuss it with God and write out a strategy to go about improving it using the priority order of TECRM principles.

Day 27

How to Make Disciples using TECRM

Yesterday we looked at how to use The Empowered Christian Road Map for life improvement. Remember, we don't exist just to have a good life. We exist to glorify God and make disciples of Jesus. Today we're going to look at ways you could use this map to help you improve at making disciples.

OVERVIEW OF THE EMPOWERED CHRISTIAN ROAD MAP

1. *The Right Road Map* - All that you do moves you toward the right destination (eternal life w/ Jesus)
2. *Rebuilt and Headed In New Direction* - You're repentant, saved by grace through faith, born again
3. *Dump the Garbage Baggage* - You're dedicated to spiritual freedom, restoration and sanctification
4. *The Atmosphere In The Car* - You're renewing and managing your thoughts, beliefs and emotions
5. *The New Direction Is Fruitful* - You're dedicated to bearing more good internal and external fruit

6. *Your Mission As Disciple* - You're embracing an eternal-minded and gospel-centered purpose
7. *The Auto Club (The Church)* - You're partnering with others in a local church in unity and purpose
8. *Same Destination, Alternate Routes* - You're embracing your unique testimony, identity and calling

Next, we'll examine 3 types of believers and how these principles can help you disciple them.

PERSON "A" - UNSAVED OR CULTURAL CHRISTIAN

Has this happened to you? So there you are, talking with someone who just told you they're on the verge of losing their job. They're also upset because their relative was just diagnosed with a serious disease. Before you've even had an opportunity to respond to either of these things they change the subject and start complaining about something the opposing political party is doing. In exasperation they exclaim: the world sucks, I feel lost, I have no idea what to do, I'm just going to go get drunk!

What do you do? How do you make a positive effect in this person's life right now? Do you just randomly pick something they said and start there? Do you just pick the thing that they are the most upset about? Or maybe pick the thing that seems the most important to you? With so many things to respond to, which one was even the most important?

Well, according to Biblical Christianity, none of the above! Remember principle #1: the right road map. The truth is that none of those issues affected their eternal destination. And if even you could solve every single one of them, if they're not saved, and still destined to Hell, what did you really do for them? All you did was make this life a little better before they spent eternity separated from God. That's hardly the ideal outcome.

I recommend gently, but assertively, interrupting their hopeless ranting and current pattern of thinking and interjecting an entirely new focus and direction. Ask them something like, "Hey, this might sound way off topic but hear me out. If you died today are you confident that you would go to Heaven?"

Anything but a quick, resounding "yes" means that you should share the gospel with them, see if they're willing to repent of their sins and receive Jesus as their Lord and Savior. Now it's possible they may say they don't care about this, or perhaps you know them well enough that you've already brought this subject up other times and you know they are very opposed to this topic. In that case you could skip this step. But still notice that this is the most important step. Whenever we have the opportunity to, it's best to always start with principles #1 and 2.

If they had answered yes already, or had made the decision to trust Jesus after you asked, this is a great place to start from with their other problems. Now this person has their most urgent and important problem solved. They can now pan out and see all of their other issues in light of the big picture of eternal life, and they can have gratitude, clarity, peace, joy, and hope as they work through the remaining issues. They also now have God and the church to help with them.

PERSON "B" - THE IMMATURE BELIEVER

They're already born again and saved, so you wouldn't need to start with principles #1 and 2, right? Yes, that is unless they're struggling with doubts, they lack understanding of right doctrine, or they're having some other crisis of faith. But it's often still good to start there anyways.

All believers, especially immature ones, benefit from being reminded core truths. This is especially true during difficult situations and it's a good preliminary safeguard. Unless you know they are saved for sure, don't assume that they're saved just because you've assumed it or even because they're in a church gathering.

It's always a good starting point in the discipleship process. Then just proceed chronologically through the principles. Most of the time you can follow this exact order of importance and prioritize accordingly.

Removal of demonic lies and toward freedom and sanctification (principle #3) comes before teaching them how to evangelize and make disciples (principle #6). If you have them making disciples without them walking in freedom and holiness what kind of disciples would they make!?

Likewise with their need to grow first in their ability to manage their own thoughts, beliefs, and feelings (principle #4) before coming together to serve in any large capacity within the church (principle #7). How much more damage will they cause other people in the church if they're prematurely trying to work with others in mission but can't even manage themselves yet!?

The same is true in regards to them first prioritizing having a righteous and fruitful home life (principle #5), and being obedient to the general, universal purpose that all believers have in common (principle #6), before focusing on their unique gifting and calling (principle #8).

The principles are not completed one-at-a-time in sequential order, but they are prioritized in order of importance because they do build upon each other. As you're discipling people, ask them deep questions to really get to know them and understand their life. This way, even though they're always growing a little bit in all 8 principles, you can know which principle area to help them give most of their focus to right now.

PERSON "C" - THE DEDICATED DISCIPLE

They're already holy, mature, and dedicated, aren't they done? Haha! No, to be a disciple means to be like the one we're following: Jesus. This means we're never finished. There will always be room for more personal growth, deeper intimacy with God, closer alignment with His will, and greater empowerment and utilization of our lives towards the fulfillment of bringing His kingdom to earth. None of us is as much like Jesus as we could be.

The further along disciples are, the more they're to be trained to lead in greater capacities, eldership, deaconship, to help disciple others through this same process. Discipling them means to help them more fully embrace their gospel-centered purpose (principle #6), to help more Person A's become Person B's and Person B's become Person C's.

Your goal is to help them increase their involvement or leadership responsibilities in the church (principle #7), and more fully utilize and embrace their unique identity and calling (principle #8).

Discipleship is an ongoing process, not a one-size-fits-all program. How you help people move from A to B to C, from being unsaved to being a fully mobilized disciple, will vary from person to person. These 8 principles will help serve as foundational guide posts while monitoring their progress and addressing their unique needs. Tomorrow we'll look at how this framework can help remove confusion or distraction and make progress towards making better life decisions to designing a life plan and fulfill your calling.

PRAYER

Heavenly Father, please bring the people you want me to disciple into my life. Help me use these principles to make them more like Jesus and to advance your Kingdom. In Jesus' name. Amen.

JOURNAL

1. Who can you identify in your life as a Person A, Person B, and Person C? Talk with God and ask Him to highlight certain people that He would have you practice your discipleship with. Write down your conversation.

2. What are some friendly social ways you could connect with them this week? Ask God to give you knowledge and wisdom. Reach out in love and a desire to build the relationship and just get together. You can wait until you're in person to bring up these other important topics.

3. Reach out to all three people today and begin a conversation that leads to you somehow being in their life in a greater capacity to ultimately do what you can to help them grow in their relationship with Jesus.

Day 28

How to Make Better Decisions using TECRM

Yesterday we looked at how to use The Empowered Christian Road Map to make disciples of Jesus. Today we'll examine two different case studies to show you how this framework can help you make better life decisions that glorify God and fulfill your calling.

MAKE DECISIONS IN KEEPING WITH THE 8 PRINCIPLES

1. *The Right Road Map* - Does this bring me/us towards the right destination, eternal life with Jesus? Which option is more eternally-minded? Which would be rewarded greater treasures in Heaven?

2. *Rebuilt and Headed In New Direction* - Is this in accord with a righteous lifestyle? Am I being led by my flesh to pursue selfish worldly things or by the Holy Spirit to glorify God in this endeavor?

3. *Dump the Garbage Baggage* - Am I intentionally choosing to do this by godly wisdom? Could this desire be influenced by demons, sin, curses, bad habits, unforgiveness, or unhealed past wounds?

4. *The Atmosphere In The Car* - Is this in accord with the fruit of the Spirit? Am I directing my own thoughts, beliefs, emotions and

behavior? Do I feel a peace from God about proceeding in this?

5. *The New Direction Is Fruitful* - Which option brings me/us towards a more fruitful direction? Which is more righteous, just, helpful or beneficial? Which option is more Jesus, gospel and faith-centered?

6. *Your Mission As Disciple* - Which is in line with my gospel-centered purpose and mission? Which is permissible, yet more about comfort and pleasure? Which option is what Jesus did or would do?

7. *The Auto Club (The Church)* - Which option brings me/us towards greater partnership in unity and purpose with the global church? Which prioritizes connection and commitment in my local church?

8. *Same Destination, Alternate Routes* - Which option better embraces all of the other principles while also utilizing my unique testimony, identity, preferences, passions, talents, gifting and calling?

These principles serve as foundational guide posts reducing confusion and distractions. Prayerfully filter your difficult decisions through them and you will better align yourself with God's will and your calling. Next, we'll go through a few case studies to illustrate how to apply these principles.

CASE STUDY #1 - SHOULD I TAKE JOB? MAYBE MY CALLING!

"I just received a job offer for a new position. I'd really enjoy it and it pays double my current salary! The problem is that it's in another state so we'd have to sell our home. We do have equity so we'd make good money. Moving would be hard on our ten-year-old though since she has a hard time fitting in and making friends, and she'd have to leave her school and best friend. And the whole family would greatly miss our church. They're like close family to us. We've been there for years, really helping to impact our city. I do like my current job and we're all actually pretty happy right now but I wonder if God is calling me to move? I have always wanted to live in the mountains. Plus, there is a church nearby that we could go to. What should I do?"

What do you think? What advice would you give? What were his primary reasons provided for considering this job?

Was it primarily to glorify God (principle #1), pursue greater treasure in Heaven (principle #2), increase fruitfulness (principle #5), advance the gospel (principle #6), build up the church (principle #7), or utilize his unique attributes to advance God's kingdom (principle #8)?

No, on every account. The primary and only incentives are money and pleasure-based. The lure of a doubled salary, the financial windfall of selling their home, and the fun of living in the mountains. Now, these desires are not inherently sinful. However, making key life decisions motivated primarily by worldly pleasure is almost always the wrong direction to go in.

And then when you factor in that this pursuit would be at the expense of the entire family's spiritual life, and the well being of his daughter socially, then it is sinful. What God cares most about is not prioritized in his mind at all.

Also, notice at the end he mentioned the nearby church they could go to. Christians often put a "Christian veneer" on options like that. It's a way of appeasing their own conscience, sprinkling on a little spirituality so it feels a little less bad and less like you won't be worse off spiritually as a result of doing whatever it is that you're thinking about doing.

The truth is that not every church is a good church or even one you'll enjoy. And even if it were, you're still starting from scratch and it will take a lot of time and effort to hopefully build the close relationships like the ones you've left behind. As though deep, personal friendships are a dime-a-dozen and come easily. As though more money will add greater fulfillment to your life than people! Such a lie from the pit of Hell.

No part of this decision has anything to do with moving because they felt God calling them to be a part of that specific church for a specific mission. That would be a legitimate good reason but it wasn't his real reason. So, moving is not prioritizing the spiritual health of yourself or your family, church, or community.

The reality is that this offer is likely not a gift or call from God. It's more likely a distraction from Satan to entice you and harm your family and church.

CASE STUDY #2 - SHOULD I DATE HIM? HE COULD BE THE ONE!

> "I started dating one of my exes again recently. We dated years ago, before I was a Christian. We used to sleep together. He still gets high and drunk but not as much, not like he used to. He doesn't believe or go to church but he does believe in a higher power. He said he would try coming to church with me if it's really important to me. God may want to use me to bring him to Jesus. And he could be the one! What do you think I should do?"

Well, will giving part of her heart, time, and life to a sinful nonbeliever improve her relationship with Jesus (principle #1)? No. Will being with him help her live righteously and be more Spirit-led (principle #2)? No. In fact, not only is dating an unbeliever unwise, it's also actually sinful and disobedient to the teaching found in 2 Corinthians 6:14.

Will he help her avoid being influenced by sinful temptation or demonic lies (principle #3)? No, quite the contrary. The fact that he's not as bad as he used to be is still somewhat irrelevant. That is just "bargaining" language. Presumably their past sexual history together, and his current desire to return to sleeping together outside of marriage will only cause conflict later. The same is true of him still getting drunk and high.

Will her dating and being around an unbeliever on a regular basis help her have more consistent biblical thinking and emotions and be more led by the Holy Spirit (principle #4)? Will it help her bear more good fruit with her life (principle #5)? No. The more she is around a person with an unbiblical worldview, a sinful nature, not led by the Spirit, and not led by a desire to please God, these things will all create opposition of agenda and conflict.

Will her dating an unbeliever who is reluctant to go to church at all empower her to spend more time on mission as a disciple (principle #6), increase her activity and involvement with the church (principle #7), or help her pursue her calling for Jesus (principle #8)? No to all of them! He will always be pulling away from all of these things. He may not do it maliciously or even intentionally, but it will still happen.

We're always moving. We're either moving towards God or away from Him. This is why we're not to be unequally yoked with unbelievers. If you're connected to someone you're going to fight about which direction to go in. Either changing the other person, or more likely just having conflict and compromise for both people.

God did not send him to her to date him. She can proclaim Jesus to him just fine without dating him. Satan likely sent him to use him like a pawn to tempt her to return to her sinful ways to destroy her. She should invite him to the church or other community activities. If he decides to give his life to Jesus and she sees the genuine change in him over time, then she could revisit the possibility of dating him in the future.

PRAYER

Heavenly Father, help me remember these 8 principles to make godlier and wiser decisions. Lead me by Your Spirit to become all that I can be for Your glory. In Jesus' name. Amen.

JOURNAL

1. What's an important current or future life decision you have to make? What options are available to choose from? If not your own, perhaps a loved one needing help with a decision?

2. Talk to God about it. Use the principles to analyze it deeper. List different questions and what principles it applies to.

3. Write out and assess your answers to all those questions. Which answer is a better solution that conforms best to the TECRM criteria? Has this helped you make a wiser and godlier decision?

Day 29

How to Prioritize Your Life using TECRM

Over the past few days we've looked at how to use The Empowered Christian Road Map framework to improve your life, make disciples, and make better life decisions. This lesson we're going to look at how you can use this framework to better prioritize things in your life.

The map itself is already in the right order. This lesson explains why this order is best. Then all you need to do is apply it accordingly to your situations.

PRIORITY #1 - THE RIGHT ROAD MAP

The most important things to prioritize are that which pertains to life or death, saved or unsaved, Heaven or Hell. Everything else is about improving this life, getting more accomplished in this life, getting more enjoyment out of this life. But even when good, this life is still temporary. Compared to eternity this life is like a breath. Putting anything else before these things is like trying to arrange the chairs on the Titanic. It may help improve things in the short run but in the final analysis it won't matter at all. Ask yourself,

Possible Journal Question: "Will this affect the ultimate bottom line? Does this bring me/us towards the right destination, eternal life with Jesus—or away from that?"

PRIORITY #2 - REBUILT AND HEADED IN NEW DIRECTION

This is about how we do principle one. We must be born again, a child of God. We must live righteously, but not just obeying God's Law in our own strength. Prioritizing eternal things means growing in your knowing God. This will shift your insight of what He actually wants and that will affect what you pursue, and how you pursue it.

Prioritize the different ways that help you become more like Jesus, build your faith and trust in God, and develop deeper intimacy with Him. Make sure that you're not being led by your flesh to pursue selfish worldly things, but by the Spirit to use your time, talent, and treasure to glorify God with your existence. Ask yourself,

Possible Journal Question: "Will this bring me/us to closer intimacy with God? Will this strengthen our relationship?"

PRIORITY #3 - DUMP THE GARBAGE BAGGAGE

You might think being more like Jesus means you should start with apologetics, evangelism, serving in church, etc. but it doesn't. The truth is that God wants you more than what He wants what you can do for Him.

Before Jesus even began His ministry, preaching, miracles, or anything else He did for God, the Father said, "This is my Son, whom I love; with him I am well pleased." (Matt. 3:17)

He was pleased with who He was, before anything He had done. Likewise, you need to prioritize who you are, over what you do.

Prioritize your sanctification and pursue spiritual freedom, holiness, righteousness, love and emotional wholeness. Learn biblical truth to correct demonic lies you had believed, cast out your demons, remove ungodly connections, break the curses over you, overcome your bad habits, forgive your offenders, and let God heal your wounds. Ask yourself,

> *Possible Journal Question: "Will this help me to have greater personal spiritual freedom, healing, wholeness, or growth?"*

PRIORITY #4 - THE ATMOSPHERE IN THE CAR

Next, prioritize managing your thoughts, beliefs, and emotions. This is important because who you are is what you repeatedly do. And what you do, is caused by how you feel, which is caused by what you believe, about what you are allowing yourself to think about.

Before you can have any measure of external fruitfulness in your home or community get your "inner self" in order first. Ask yourself,

> *Possible Journal Question: "Do I direct my own thoughts, beliefs, emotions, and behavior? And are they consistent with biblical gospel truth and the fruit of the Spirit?"*

PRIORITY #5 - THE NEW DIRECTION IS FRUITFUL

When you're able to direct your thoughts and behavior you can pursue a life of fruitfulness. This one also has 5 levels and their order of priority.

1. *Level 1* is Individual Internal Change through inward repentance, personal private victory over sin, character growth and development.
2. *Level 2* is Individual External Change, all behavior that affects others. This should also take the inside-out approach. First improving yourself in your marriage, then as parent, group member, church member, coworker, etc.
3. *Level 3* is creating Community Impact working with others through organized local action programs.
4. *Level 4* is Systemic Change through communities working together to promote biblical justice.
5. *Level 5* is Societal Change by communities and systems working

together towards social or global reform. Prioritize these in this order, starting in level 1, asking yourself,

Possible Journal Question: "Honestly, which level needs my attention right now?"

PRIORITY #6 - YOUR MISSION AS DISCIPLE

While God loves us as a child no matter what, and calls us to bear good fruit with our lives (Eph. 2:10), these aren't our only purpose. Jesus has also left us with a mission as His disciples to continue the work that He started. So next prioritize your universal and common calling to preach the gospel, make disciples, and advance God's kingdom on earth. Ask yourself,

Possible Journal Question: "What is more in line with my gospel-centered mission? What would Jesus do?"

PRIORITY #7 - THE AUTO CLUB (THE CHURCH)

God commands us to not forsake coming together in church community. It's also where we will get most of our direction, healing and growth, and fulfill our disciple-mission responsibilities. Ask yourself,

Possible Journal Question: "What brings greater partnership in unity and purpose in the global church? And what prioritizes connection and commitment to my local church?"

PRIORITY #8 - SAME DESTINATION, ALTERNATE ROUTES

So many people are obsessed pursuing or worrying about what should be their unique secondary calling when they're not even first fulfilling their common and primary calling as a disciple.

Likewise, it's misguided when people are worrying about the global church when they're not first a part of and helping in their local church.

First, prioritize those. Then, the final step is to ask yourself,

> *Possible Journal Question: "Will this opportunity also utilize my unique testimony, identity, preferences, passions, talents, giftings, and make me happy and fulfilled?"*

CONCLUSION

These 8 principles are not to be completed one at a time in sequential order. You should always be growing in all 8 principles simultaneously. But, since they all build upon one another, they've been prioritized in this order of importance. Remember them so you can wisely know what God would direct you to give your focus and effort to at any stage or challenge during your Christian journey.

PRAYER

Heavenly Father, help me remember these 8 principles and prioritize my life accordingly. Lead me Jesus by Your Holy Spirit to become all that I can be for Your glory. In Jesus' name. Amen.

JOURNAL

1. Talk to God about the big pieces of your life. How would you rate yourself in how well you're prioritizing the right things? What are you still giving more attention than you should be?

2. Write out the big roles, areas, and responsibilities, and the dreams you have. Order them according to their level of new priority, and list why they are in the best order of importance.

3. Spend time in prayer asking the Father to give you more of the fullness of this in your life starting now. Ask Him for wisdom, insight, and SMART ways to start living it out today.

Day 30

God's Answer to Your "Why?" (Fan or Disciple?)

Congrats! You've made it to the final day.

What should you be doing? What's God's will for your life?

People are always asking me questions like: Should I move to that city? Buy this house? Take that job? Date or marry this person? Which direction should I proceed in? Not to mention the many times God allows us to go through difficult trials, leaving us asking: Why God? why? Why so many options?

God often gives us many options to choose from in life. And rarely will we have absolute certainty that we know what the absolutely correct and best decision is. But remember this important truth: If you always focus on doing the main two things then most of the time those other secondary details don't really matter. This lesson you'll learn those two main things.

FIRST, WHAT'S GOD'S WILL FOR YOUR LIFE?

Right before His ascension into Heaven Jesus gave His final marching orders to His followers. Matthew 28:18-20 He said,

DAY 30 - GOD'S ANSWER TO YOUR "WHY?" (FAN OR DISCIPLE?)

> *"All authority in heaven and on earth has been given to me. Therefore go and make disciples of all nations, baptizing them in the name of the Father and of the Son and of the Holy Spirit, and teaching them to obey everything I have commanded you. And surely I am with you always, to the very end of the age."*

Did you catch that? Because it tells you exactly what you're to here to do. The two main things. You're to BE a disciple of Jesus who MAKES more disciples of Jesus. Sound simple enough? It is!

IT'S EASY TO BE A FAN

Before we discuss those two main things I want to ask you something real quick. Do you watch sporting events? It can be fun to gather with friends and other fans and watch your favorite sports team play. If you're not huge into sports perhaps you enjoy the theater, concerts, plays, performance art, movies, etc. The same principle applies. In all of these recreational activities the majority of the people involved are in the audience. They're the fans.

Many fans invest a lot of time to go watch their team play live, even making an entire day outing out of it. Many fans spend a lot of money as well to purchase good seats or to collect memorabilia to display around their homes. Many fans like to wear the jersey of their favorite player, hats, or other clothing items with their favorite team's logo on it.

Some fans go all out in an outlandish way, painting their faces or creating costumes with their team's colors to show their support. Many fans get very emotionally invested in the team and games. Many have an instant common-bond with other fans. This instant camaraderie may be expressed through one fan giving a "high five" after a good play to a total stranger that's also a fan of the same team. They feel like they are involved and part of the same team.

In their excitement, they may cheer on the team yelling "Go! Come on! You're almost there!" They're in a good mood when their team is winning and in a bad mood when their team is losing. Fans often identify with the team as something that they're a part of; the team being an extension of who they are. They may say things like, "We won, We lost, that player lost the game for Us."

Fans may do all of these things and more, but do you know the one thing that they will never do? Play the actual game! Despite all of their investment of their time, their money, their identity, their emotions, and more, with the sport and the team, at the end of the day they're still just a fan. Their participation in the game and the team is just an illusion.

MAIN THING #1 - BE A DISCIPLE OF JESUS IN THE GAME

Sometimes people treat being a Christian this way. Like a fan on the sideline just watching. But Jesus doesn't give us this option. If you're not in the game for Jesus you're still kind of on Satan's team. Jesus calls every follower of His to get off their seat and get in the game!

FANS WATCH. DISCIPLES PLAY THE GAME.

Since you're actually going to be in the game you need to get involved and invested at a much deeper level. You need to know your captain, Jesus. Jesus commanded you to teach them (the disciples that you're going to make)—everything He commanded you. So, you need to know the truth, His Word (the Bible), and what's important to Him.

Jesus said we haven't been left as orphans (John 14:18). He's with us always; so you need to know Him personally, too. Fans still live for themselves. Their participation and support is an illusion. They can leave the game early if their team is losing or turn off the TV if they don't feel like watching anymore. The game will still go on.

Some people are extremely superstitious about sports. They think if they wear their lucky shirt that's never been washed, or follow the same ritual before every game it somehow it will help the stars align and their team will win. It's a sense of purpose, of meaning, a way to feel involved, like they're a part of the game and contributing to something bigger than themselves. It's just superstitious nonsense. It's all an illusion. The truth is your just a fan and nothing you do makes any difference in the outcome of the actual game.

Some fans even switch team allegiances, based on how well they're doing, or they'll love a player while he's part of their team but then hate that same person if he transfers to a rival team. The love and allegiance of fans is superficial. Unlike this form of fake love and support, disciples die to themselves in order to live for Christ (2 Cor. 5:15). They're all in. There is no team switching. You can't just support Jesus when it seems like doing so will improve your life and then choose not to when it gets difficult. There is no alternative. There's Jesus and life and there's Satan and death.

Disciples of Jesus surrender their will to follow Him to become a "living sacrifice" for God (Rom. 12:1). Fans sit in the stands arrogantly boasting that they know the best plays to do. They often live the illusion that they're not only one of the players but also the head coach. This is another form of disillusionment. Not only are they not an elite athlete playing at the highest levels of their game, they're also not an educated and experienced coach of the game or of athletes. Yet, many believe that they are. Sorry sports fans, I'm not trying to pick on you, I'm just telling you how it is. I mainly just want to make sure you're not committing the same errors with your faith!

Do you complain about how wrong other churches do things? Are you involved and actually participating in doing all the right things at your church?Do you see how some people street preach and share the gospel and look down on their wrong approach? Are you sharing the gospel in a more effective way?Stop judging from the outside. Get in the game. You will realize it may be harder than you think once you're actually involved. At the very least you'll give other people more grace. At best you can discover what actually does work best for the Kingdom and help teach others what you've learned. Then you'll be a part of the solution, actually in the game, instead of a part of the problem, just complaining as a supposed-know-it-all from the stands!

Disciples of Jesus must trust Jesus as their head coach. They must execute the plays He provides without second guessing Him. And when the game looks grim and, by worldly standards, like we're losing, disciples must know that He is Lord of lords, in control, remains faithful, and His way is always best.

Just like in sports, it's the responsibility of each player to do their part well, not to focus on what the other players are or aren't doing. The coach worries about the cohesiveness of the rest of the team. The players need to perform well, know the plays, follow instructions, and execute their own plays well.

Likewise, disciples need to listen and obey Jesus or His plays on the field won't be executed properly. They need to know and submit to God's Word and the prompting and direction of the Holy Spirit.

Fans sit in the stands, get drunk, eat junk food, getting fat and lazy. But not the players. They are elite athletes that have to train hard, remain disciplined, and always training to improve and keep developing their skill. They need to not only perform their own plays well, they need to be a good team player.

The "main thing" you need to do in life is BE a disciple of Jesus. So get your own house in order first. Your personal relationship with God and your spiritual condition is your priority. God wants YOU more than what He can do through you for others. Discipline yourself and get in the game.

MAIN THING #2 - MAKE DISCIPLES OF JESUS

Now that you have a clear picture of what it takes be a disciple instead of a fan the second main thing Jesus said is go and make MORE disciples.

This is why you need to start with yourself. The people we reach, need to see our authenticity and sincerity if they're going to believe in what we're doing and forsake their old lives to join and follow Jesus with us. If we're not genuine, we're going to look like hypocritical whitewashed tombs: outwardly clean and religious but inwardly dead and never transformed by the gospel reality.

Your job is not to make disciples, as though you're the one forcing them to be a disciple even when they don't really want to be one. Think "make disciples" more as "help them to become disciples." Your job is to deliver the message of the gospel, believe and teach the truths of the faith, and walk alongside them helping them to trust and follow Jesus in the same ways that you already are. Mark 16:15 Jesus said,

> "Go into all the world and preach the gospel to all creation."

2 Corinthians 5:18-20 says God,

> "God was reconciling the world to himself in Christ, not counting people's sins against them. And he has committed to us the message of reconciliation. We are therefore Christ's ambassadors, as though God were making his appeal through us."

What we have is very good news! Realize you're a letter messenger for Jesus's team being sent to invite others to get off the sideline, join the team, and get in the game. Are you delivering it and inviting others to join? Are you showing them the difference between being a fan and a disciple? Are you in the game modeling what it looks like? Once they're on the team your job is to be a good teammate and help everyone play their best. Train the rest of the team to invite others and help them as well.

PRAYER

LORD God, thank You for giving my life eternal purpose, to know You forever and help others do the same. By Your Spirit, transform me into a mighty disciple that makes more disciples. In Jesus' name. Amen.

JOURNAL

1. What are ways you're guilty of being a fan? There's no condemnation, but God does want you to grow and learn from it.

2. What are ways you will live more like a disciple, starting today?

3. What's the purpose of your life?

Endnotes

1. Piper, John, "What's the Origin of Desiring God's Slogan?," 20 Sept. 2017, desiringgod.org/interviews/whats-the-origin-of-desiring-gods-slogan, Accessed 27 August, 2023.

2. BrainyQuote, "Viktor E. Frankl Quotes," , https://brainyquote.com/quotes/viktor_e_frankl_131417, Accessed 27 August 2023.

3. McDaniel, Lori, "Five Inspirational Quotes For Life On Mission," 23 March 2015, namb.net/planter-wives-blog/five-inspirational-quotes-for-life-on-mission/, Accessed 28, August 2023.

4. Mueller, Steve, "'Zig Ziglar Quote' - The 30 Most Inspiring Focus Quotes," , planetofsuccess.com/blog/2016/inspiring-focus-quotes/, Accessed 27 August 2023.

5. GoodReads, "Quote by Andy Andrews," GoodReads.com, https://www.goodreads.com/quotes/188679-despite-popular-belief-to-the-contrary-there-is-absolutely-no, Accessed 27 August, 2023.

6. Durant, Will, "Will Durant Quote," PlanetofSuccess.com, planetofsuccess.com/blog/2016/inspiring-focus-quotes/, Accessed 27 August, 2023.

7. Sweatt, Lydia, "18 Motivational Quotes About Successful Goal Setting," Success.com, 29 December 2016, success.com/18-motivational-quotes-about-successful-goal-setting/, Accessed 27 August 2023.

8. Sweatt, Lydia, "18 Motivational Quotes About Successful Goal Setting," Success.com, 29 December 2016, success.com/18-motivational-quotes-about-successful-goal-setting/, Accessed 27 August 2023.

Afterword

I hope this 30-day devotional has enriched your life! If you enjoyed it, it would help a ton if you please leave it a review at Amazon. https://MPoweredChristian.org/Amazon

I want to encourage you not to let up but continue to press in deeper and keep going! Here are six ways you could continue to the next level:

1. Begin your next 30-day devotional. Browse my other 4D Devotionals at: https://MPoweredChristian.org/4D-Devotionals

2. Enjoyed learning about the ideas in The Empowered Christian Road Map? It's available in standard or color paperback, Kindle, Nook, ebook, PDF, and audiobook. Discounted versions and lots of FREE resources here: https://MPoweredChristian.org/TECRM

3. Get advice, personal counseling, life coaching, or ministry training directly from Pastor Brian (offered worldwide over Zoom). Learn more at: https://MPoweredChristian.org/Coaching

4. Enroll in The Empowered Christian Road Map Transformation Program, a 6-month, 200-training hour virtual DIY program that combines the book, 50+ videos, assignments, 30+ quizzes, one-on-one Zoom sessions with Pastor Brian. Earns a professional certificate. Learn more at https://MPoweredChristian.org/TECRMTP

5. FREE - 200+ videos on my YouTube channel. Start watching now at: https://MPoweredChristian.org/YouTube

6. FREE - 4,000+ questions answered on our Quora channel. Start reading now at: https://MPoweredChristian.org/Quora

Road Map Resources

To assist you in cross-referencing certain devotionals you enjoyed with those topics in the other The Empowered Christian Road Map resources they've been outlined below for your convenience. Go here for discounted books and FREE resources: https://MPoweredChristian.org/TECRM

CHAPTER 1 - RECALCULATING... THE RIGHT ROAD MAP

Day 3 - What's The Purpose Of Life?
Day 4 - You've Been Given An Incredible Opportunity!
Day 5 - A Final Destination Worth Striving Toward

CHAPTER 2 - REBUILT AND HEADED IN A NEW DIRECTION

Day 6 - Why You Must Be Born Again To Be Saved
Day 7 - Understanding The Process Of Salvation
Day 8 - What Does It Mean To Be A New Creation In Christ?

CHAPTER 3 - DUMPING THE GARBAGE BAGGAGE

Day 9 - How Satan Is The Saboteur Of Your Journey
Day 10 - The Four Main Ways Satan Leads People To Hell
Day 11 - Close These 8 Open Doors And Keep Satan Out

CHAPTER 4 - THE ATMOSPHERE IN THE CAR

Day 12 - 8 Keys To A Mindset For Emotional Health And Success
Day 13 - The 4 Habits Of The Emotionally Resilient Christian
Day 14 - 8 Lifestyle Behaviors Of The Emotionally Resilient Christian

CHAPTER 5 - THE NEW DIRECTION IS VERY FRUITFUL

Day 15 - The Fruitfulness Of Your Life Shows Your Direction
Day 16 - God Demands Moral Righteousness And Justice
Day 17 - Are Your Good Works Actually Evidence of Saving Faith?

CHAPTER 6 - OUR MISSION AS DISCIPLES

Day 18 - The Christian Mission Is Not To Fix The World
Day 19 - Your Mission As A Disciple Of Jesus
Day 20 - 4 Keys To Run Your Spiritual Race Well

CHAPTER 7 - THE AUTO CLUB (THE CHURCH)

Day 21 - Who And What Is The Church?
Day 22 - What Are The Basic Functions Of The Local Church?
Day 23 - How To Go From Healthy To Empowered Church

CHAPTER 8 - SAME DESTINATION, ALTERNATE ROUTES

Day 24 - What's Your Identity and Calling?
Day 25 - How To Be Empowered For Your Mission

THESE LESSONS WERE ALL AIMLESS EXCLUSIVES!

Day 1 - Where Is Your Life Going?
Day 2 - The Empowered Christian Road Map - Your Life Blueprint
Day 26 - How To Improve Your Life Using TECRM
Day 27 - How To Make Disciples Using TECRM
Day 28 - How To Make Better Decisions Using TECRM
Day 29 - How To Prioritize Your Life Using TECRM
Day 30 - God's Answer To Your "Why?" (Fan or Disciple?)

www.ingramcontent.com/pod-product-compliance
Lightning Source LLC
LaVergne TN
LVHW051520070426
835507LV00023B/3213